LIFE
AFTER
DIVORCE

REVISED & UPDATED

LIFE AFTER DIVORCE

Create a New Beginning

Sharon Wegscheider-Cruse

Health Communications, Inc.
Deerfield Beach, Florida

www.hcibooks.com

Library of Congress Cataloging-in-Publication Data

Wegscheider-Cruse, Sharon, 1938-
   Life after divorce : create a new beginning / Sharon Wegscheider-Cruse.—Rev.
& updated.
     p. cm.
   Includes bibliographical references.
   ISBN 978-0-7573-1667-8 (pbk.)
   ISBN 0-7573-1667-0 (pbk.)
   ISBN 978-0-7573-1668-5 (epub)
   ISBN 0-7573-1668-9 (epub)
   1. Divorce.   2. Divorce counseling.   3. Divorced people—Counseling of.
I. Title.
   HQ814.W44 2012
   306.89—dc23

                                   2012040348

Publisher: Health Communications, Inc.
          3201 S.W. 15th Street
          Deerfield Beach, FL 33442-8190

Cover design by Dane Wesolko
Interior design and formatting by Dawn Von Strolley Grove

Other Books by Sharon Wegscheider-Cruse

Another Chance: Hope and Health for the Alcoholic Family

Calling All Women: From Competition to Connection

*Choicemaking: For Spirituality Seekers, Co-Dependents
    and Adult Children*

Coupleship: How to Build a Relationship

Dancing with Destiny: Turning Points on the Journey of Life

Girl Talk: Daily Reflections for Women of All Ages

*Grandparenting: A Guide for Today's Grandparents with
    over 50 Activities to Strengthen One of Life's
    Most Powerful and Rewarding Bonds*

*Learning to Balance Your Life: 6 Powers to Restore
    Your Energy and Spirit*

Learning to Love Yourself: Finding Your Self-Worth

*Learning to Love Yourself, Revised & Updated:
    Finding Your Self-Worth*

*The Miracle of Recovery: Healing for Addicts,
    Adult Children and Co-Dependents*

Understanding Codependency, Updated and Expanded

Thank you to the many couples
who have worked and shared
in the Onsite Couples Program.
The combination of life stories from
both the staff and the participants
has created a body of knowledge
that has enhanced the lives of many couples.
Also, a special thanks to Steve Rutlen,
who introduced me to the creative
and useful approach taken by those
who are making collaborative divorce
possible for couples.

Contents

Introduction

The hardest thing to learn in life is which bridge to cross and which to burn.

DAVID RUSSELL

Frequently reported near 50 percent, divorce rates have continued to climb since the original *Life After Divorce* was published. This may not be exact, but it is close. According to Jennifer Baker of the Forest Institute of Professional Psychology, 50 percent of first marriages, 67 percent of second, and 74 percent of third all end in divorce.

It is a commentary on the culture of marriage today. From each divorce come many painful fallouts, and periodically, there is a "for the better" lifestyle change.

Let me tell you about Jan, a lovely woman about fifty years old. She married almost thirty years ago. Her husband is a quiet man working in the computer industry. He has few interests, mostly passive ones such as computer games, watching sports on TV, and reading. Jan is outgoing and works for a public relations firm. She is full of energy, likes to learn new things, and is very active playing tennis and hiking.

She is currently doing all the social networking for the couple. He brings very little to their social life but enjoys her success, connections, and lifestyle. She brings in more income than he does, which allows him to keep buying technical toys. She also brings the energy into the relationship; however, Jan is tired. She feels used. Jan has been ill on and off a great deal the last couple of years. Her doctor is telling her that most of it is stress related. She cannot remember feeling appreciated or cared for in a long time.

Jan was offered a new career opportunity, and she would like to move across the country to take advantage of it. Her husband wants her to keep doing what she has always done. She wants to pursue her career—a path that offers much more give-and-take in her relationships than there is in her marriage. Jan has filed for divorce.

This example can be viewed two ways. We can dwell on the sadness surrounding the impending divorce, as there must have been a time when love was present in this relationship. Or, we can look at it from another perspective. Jan is making changes on her own behalf that will likely bring better health and joy into her life. To truly know whether the divorce is a good move or if it is about to bring even more pain, we would need to know all of the circumstances surrounding her case. This is one reason why divorce can be so confusing not only for the couple involved but for family and friends as well.

Other issues that may further complicate divorce include child custody issues and emotional struggles between both parents and adult children, all of which will be explored later. Sometimes, even grandchildren can complicate the situation.

Of the three, grandchildren issues are often some of the most difficult to face. Children bring out the protective nature of everyone involved, and each person tends to believe that his or her perspective is the correct one. Sometimes the conflict around custody and care brings out the need to control, and power struggles become paramount. Issues surrounding financial support, alcohol use, and religious beliefs, just to name a few, can also complicate the situation.

During a divorce, friends often feel that they have to choose sides. Therefore, many friendships are severed after a divorce. This fact is a sad and an unnecessary loss. Yet perhaps it doesn't have to be the case. I will address ways you can preserve friendships.

It is my hope that some of these ideas and subjects will be clarifying for you as you take this next step in your life. May this revised edition also be helpful for divorce attorneys. Many have sent letters informing me of the positive impact the original *Life After Divorce* has had on their practices and how they've recommended that their divorcing clients read it before starting negotiations.

Major Reasons for Divorce

ABUSE

Abuse can be emotional or physical. Ignoring the needs of either partner can be a painful type of emotional abuse. Withholding approval, blaming, judging, and not carrying the responsibility of a partner are all forms of emotional abuse. Becoming involved in any addiction or dependency places an emotional burden and pain on the other partner. Alcoholism, workaholism, laziness, sexually acting out, avoidance of child care, gambling, and excess spending all come with consequences and are often described as emotional abuse.

Tom works hard. He puts in seventy-hour weeks and is tired much of the time. His wife, Pam, is a spendaholic. To keep the credit cards paid, Tom must hold a second job. On Sundays, he drives a tour bus.

For a long time Tom felt guilty for not bringing in enough money to cover the credit cards. He became angry because Pam could not control her spending. He was surprised to hear a counselor tell him that he was suffering from abuse.

Kim is very overweight. She feels fat and lonely much of the time. In her marriage, she has been left solely in charge of the home front. Her life is very unhappy. John is gone most of the time, either working, playing basketball with the guys, or stopping for a beer with coworkers on most nights. He makes frequent snide remarks about his wife's weight and hints that she isn't much fun. After seeking counseling, Kim was amazed to hear the counselor say that she is being emotionally abused.

Emotional abuse is subtle, frequent, and painful. Physical abuse is very clear. It's the unwanted, physical abuse one partner acts toward the other. All forms of shoving, pushing, and hitting fall into this category. Pressuring a partner to have unwanted sex is also physical abuse. All types of abuse are an indicator that you absolutely need to seek help outside the marriage.

Life expands or shrinks in proportion to one's courage.

ANAÏS NIN

ADDICTIONS

As mentioned above, all addictions are harmful to a relationship. One in every ten marriages is affected by addiction of some kind, including chemical addictions: alcoholism, nicotine addiction, prescription drug addiction, illegal drug addiction, and food addiction; and behavior addictions: sex addiction, money addiction, work addiction, exercise addiction, sports addiction, technology addiction, and spending addiction. Addiction of any kind impacts not only the one with the behavior but the spouse as well. Again, at this point outside help becomes necessary.

LACK OF COMMUNICATION

When a couple is no longer able to communicate, separation and eventually divorce is likely. The most common concern I have heard in my practice was "I want help, but my partner won't go to counseling with me." This usually means the relationship is beyond repair. When only one person is willing to look at the situation, willing to hear the other person, and willing to make changes, there is little hope for the relationship. "Isn't there something I can do to make things better even if my partner won't join me in getting help?" Too often I had to deliver the painful news, "One person cannot get well for two." If one partner refuses to communicate in a way that brings about change in the relationship, chances are there will be a divorce.

Anger is the red light on the dashboard. What is going on underneath? What is under the hood? Anger is only a warning signal that something is wrong.

CAREER ISSUES

In today's economic times, most families are a two-career family. Careers take time, energy, and lifestyle commitments. Work in general is a major stressor in many marriages, and without good communication, it has the ability to damage relationships beyond repair.

Management of time can become an issue within itself, especially when one partner travels and the other does not. One may work days, while the other works nights. Many times one parent is left taking care of the home and the children. This can lead to many ego problems that typically arise when there is inequality in salary. Partners are often left with great resentment.

When time is not properly managed, a mixture of emotions starts to weigh heavily on both partners. Fatigue sets in and impacts sexual desire. Anger fueled by the disproportion in salary and household chores is elevated, and hurt begins to develop in the partner who takes on the burden of childcare. Proper time management is key in avoiding many of these issues. Without it, the loneliness each partner feels will continue to grow and negatively influence the amount of time spent together.

> There is only one success—to be able
> to spend your life in your own way.
>
> *VANITY FAIR*

MONEY DIFFERENCES

Money remains a big topic and an important one. Sometimes the financial difficulties last longer than the marriage and continue to cause hurt and stress for many years.

Mary is an idealistic young teacher who married Ed while they were both students in college. Ed spent money quite freely, and for awhile Mary enjoyed the travel, the nice car, and the classy apartment Ed rented. Life was good. After graduating, Mary started her teaching career and Ed decided to go for both a master's degree and then on to a doctorate. Once he completed his studies, Ed began teaching in the university system, affording him a larger salary than Mary's. Ed also had become accustomed to every kind of electronic gadget available, from computers to music. Because he made the larger salary, he felt justified in buying anything he wanted. His spending went out of control and Mary became very upset. She wanted to have children, while Ed wanted to be able to have an income stream that allowed him his purchases and adventures. They tried for three years to work out a mutual budget, but their interests and ideas were too far apart regarding money. The marriage did not make it.

> Be thankful for what you have; you'll end up having more. If you concentrate on what you don't have, you will never, ever have enough.
>
> OPRAH WINFREY

LOSS OF INTEREST

When there is a great deal of stress on a relationship, sometimes it is just easier to go it alone. Alone, one can choose how to spend time, energy, and money. Any number of reasons can cause a person to feel so overwhelmed that he or she begins to not care or respect the partner enough to try to make the relationship work. One may feel like he or she is the major contributor to the relationship. Perhaps he or she is the main or busiest caretaker of the children, the one with the largest salary, or maybe the social secretary. Sometimes people just grow apart. First they stop loving, and then they stop caring and just want out. By the time one partner feels this way, divorce is most likely inevitable. He or she gives up and believes that divorce will bring relief, even though it brings on issues of its own.

SOCIAL INTERESTS

When falling in love, people stretch their interests to help the relationship grow. She tries her hand at fishing, and he walks through the mall as she looks for just the right pair of shoes. Everything takes on meaning as they discover each other's worlds and interests. Some couples go on and develop new, joint interests while taking on interests of their own as individuals.

The problem comes when the mutual interests do not materialize and each person goes back to his or her individual ones. With busy lifestyles and limited time, either the couple places an emphasis on what they do together as a couple, or they revert to what they enjoyed when single. Jobs, children, social networking, friends, and other responsibilities can interfere with couple time, single time, or both, further contributing to the couple's diminishing intimacy. When this happens, the couple grows apart.

CHEATING

When one partner cheats and the other finds out, it is very hard to return to a place of trust. It is truly like trying to put toothpaste back into the tube. Cheating on one's partner has sadly become an epidemic in our culture. Short of one or both partners suffering from sex addiction, infidelity is usually the result of actions taken by both partners involved in a relationship. Again, as with divorce, addictions, lack of communication, financial difficulties, social interests, poor time management, and stress all play a role here.

In this book, new material has been added that expands on the latest information surrounding:

- Technology and relationships
- Divorce and friendships
- Children and divorce
- The benefits of mediation and collaboration

It is my hope that this book will be helpful to the divorcing couple, their friends, their children of all ages, and the process before, during, and after the divorce.

In times of change, learners inherit the earth,
while the learned find themselves
fully equipped to deal with a world that no longer exists.

ERIC HOFFER

1
DIVORCE POSSIBILITIES: ACTION VERSUS FEAR

*D*ivorce no longer carries its old stigma in our society, but it hurts just as much as ever. With the divorce rate as high as it is, few of us fail to cringe, at least inwardly, when the word is mentioned. Most marriages have a tinderbox with at least a few combustible issues. At frustrating times when our differences flare, just thinking about divorce may be a safety valve. But we're not serious. We'll keep the lid on and work out our problems—somehow.

Then the time comes when one-half of a couple decides that solutions to the marital problems are not going to happen. Working it out has failed. We have failed. At least, that's how we feel.

So we divorce and the marriage is over. But divorce recovery has just begun.

Is it the end of the world? Or the beginning of a better world for us, in which peace, greater fulfillment, and enhanced self-esteem aren't dreams but realities?

No one can doubt my response to that question. We're not only talking about divorce survival in this book. This is about taking hold of our experience and using it to turn our lives around.

The Event of Divorce

We're taking an event that some see as primarily negative and bending it into a life enhancer. As a result of divorce we're going to be learning so much about ourselves—and others—that we'll eventually say, "Divorce was one of the best things that ever happened to me!"

I did it. I came to a positive attitude about divorce. Many others have, too. All it takes is understanding, commitment, and, most of all, action. The ability to change also helps.

There are no "victims" of divorce in the classic sense. There are only victims of the myth that divorce is something to feel guilty about or lose confidence over. Divorce prompts a wide range of feelings: relief, anger, hope, hopelessness, sadness, excitement, shame, regret, vengefulness, pity—and almost everything in between. Divorce is about the shattering of fondest hopes and fantasies about a life partner that didn't materialize. No wonder that recovering from all of this presents the challenge of a lifetime. But it is a challenge we can accept with so much help available to us in many forms, including the often underdeveloped source, which is ourselves.

DIVORCE VARIABLES

Many variables impact each divorce. They include:

- Young children
- Older children
- Adult children
- Child support problems
- Alimony problems
- Custody problems
- Affairs and betrayals

In addition to these are a host of other issues. There are those supporters and criticizers among friends and relatives; the different perspectives of a first divorce compared with a second divorce; even variables when we talk about either short-term marriages or long-term marriages; and the "excess baggage" that we bring to a marriage from our childhood families or a previous marriage.

We could talk endlessly about how every variation complicates or simplifies divorce, but the focus of this book is on healing from the trauma that divorce presents to us. Whatever they are, the forms are not insurmountable. Our concern is: Can we surmount them? We need to know we've got what it takes, and we need to learn why it's been hidden within us. How can we bring forth our remarkable latent capacities to cope and thrive? How can we live without a spouse and like it? How do we deal with the children, the relatives, and the mutual friends? How do we keep from making other mistakes in relationships?

Our questions may be seriously tinged with self-doubt. Erasing this doubt will be our main goal.

In a perfect world, all marriages would succeed because we would all be psychic and aware of every present and future need of our own and our mate's. This book is not about promoting divorce as a means of growth, even though that is frequently the result. It is about releasing people from the past to pursue with confidence the new direction their personal lives are taking.

> Dreams come with an expiration date.
> If we don't do something about them, they either
> wither or take up residence elsewhere.
>
> *BARBARA WINTERS*

Society has been changing rapidly and radically. People change in response to it, and some marriages need to end as a result. If a divorce is going to happen, let's make it an event marking renewal not useless regret.

In addition to my twenty-plus years of working with couples and families, I have interviewed more than 200 divorced people to find out what the divorce recovery process felt like and ultimately meant to them. Some of these ex-spouses will be sharing their stories with us as we explore the challenges we face.

In talking to many people about what caused and contributed to their divorces, the number-one marriage killer was perceived to be a lack of basic emotional connection between husband and wife. When people were asked to be more specific, the most common reason cited for the end of their marriage was that one partner simply lost passion for the other.

Many of the people I interviewed said they sensed something was wrong quite early in the relationship. Half said that even though they knew something was wrong, they hung in there for four years or more, refusing to believe their marriages couldn't get better.

Here are the most frequent reasons for divorce among my surveyed ex-partners, starting with the most common problem:

1. Lack of emotional intimacy
2. Affection dissatisfaction
3. Work interference
4. Child-rearing disagreements
5. Husband's inability to accept wife's work outside the home
6. Husband's inability to make money
7. Infidelity
8. Sexual dissatisfaction
9. Boredom
10. Lack of friendship

Obviously, any of these is a serious problem to live with. No wonder happiness was the word agreed upon by half the people I surveyed in response to my question "What emotion did you feel most often after divorcing?"

All too frequently, people afraid of divorce assume that divorced people are always lonely and depressed. And those who are lonely and depressed tend to think this is the way it has to be. As my survey shows, many people are in a position to view it as a life-affirming, self-affirming change—and we all can achieve that viewpoint! That's what this book is about.

One thing most of us learn from divorce is that the experience is far more than getting over a separation and getting used to living alone. That's jumping a step. For many, divorce introduces us to ourselves, which for several years was at least partially hidden by adaptations to the needs and personality of someone else. Finding out what we would do and want if we were free to choose can be a little frightening. We've changed since before the beginning of our marriages when we were single. Who are we today? Worry about our new status can delay that discovery.

> We know that if we embrace our ideals,
> we must prove worthy of them and that
> scares [us deeply]. . . . We will lose our friends
> and family, who will no longer recognize us.
>
> *STEVE PRESSFIELD*

In all our post-divorce transactions, we need to concentrate on action more and imagining calamities less. "To thine own self be true," Shakespeare said, with good reason. When we cling to old images of ourselves or ideas of how others expect us to be, the outcome will never be positive. It's mainly through doing something about our situations that we learn how strong, how adaptable, how clever, and how capable we really are. Convincing ourselves of our positive points just by imagining them doesn't work. If you don't know who you are, you won't know where you are going. But if you don't start going, you won't start finding out who you are.

A PRACTICAL BEGINNING

Many very practical matters need to be tackled in the beginning of divorce; however, don't let the momentum of your actions wind down after you have done the following:

- Agreed on decisions affecting children
- Divided personal belongings
- Changed wills and legal documents
- Informed parents
- Informed siblings
- Informed friends
- Chosen a good accountant
- Arranged new telephone listings
- Notified the post office
- Separated the bank accounts
- Dealt with the charge accounts
- Redone the bedrooms and closets (more space!)

BECOMING SINGLE AGAIN

In this new time of being single, wonderful discoveries will be made. They include:

1. Finding out we are going to make it.
2. Finding out we can be on our own.
3. Finding out it is sort of nice to be in charge of all our time and activities.
4. Enjoying some solitude and serenity.

Some of the discoveries aren't so pleasant:

1. We miss having a meal with that person.
2. We wish there were someone to share day-to-day life with.
3. We find we keep running into certain sadnesses—some shortfalls and habits we don't like—over and over again.
4. We don't have the other person to blame.
5. Eventually, we have to confront the fact that we alone are responsible for what is happening to us and what is going to happen. No more leaning on another's life.

Full singleness does not occur at the same moment for both of the separating spouses. Both may be working at it, both in transition, but they end their process of divorce recovery at different times. Some people may remarry immediately. Some, eventually. Some are going to love being single and vow never to give up their in-charge feelings again. Comparing your feelings and actions with your ex-partner's or someone else's is not valid. We need to see ourselves as unique and on our own.

Today, I myself am in a marriage that is fulfilling, challenging, and of great value to me. There was a time when I did not believe this would ever happen to me. That was when I was living in the past.

If we are to be fully alive, we will actively live with changes our whole lives. Things will not remain in static pain or static peace. Life is not like that. It is constantly moving, surrounded by movement. If you go with it, instead of trying to swim against the current, you can have a fantastic journey and adventure. Repeat the following mantra to yourself.

I release my past and former relationships. Today is the only day that really exists. The past is gone. The only place it exists is in my own thoughts. When I let the past become very powerful, the hurt of the past, the mistakes of the past—sometimes even the joys of the past— make me miss out on what's happening today.

Nothing will make the past the present. Dwelling on it drains energy I could be using to focus on the present. I won't forget it, but I will say good-bye to it. From what it has taught me, I will fashion a key to the future—a tool only to help me, not to hinder me. I'm not who I was yesterday; I'm not who I will be—but I'm getting there a day at a time—lighter and self-powered!

2

DYNAMICS OF A DISSOLVING MARRIAGE

*J*oan, Ken, Kathy, and Bob experienced divorce from the perspectives of four different lives. Throughout the book we will follow their stories, from guilt, doubt, and resentment, through the process of self-understanding to new lives of self-fulfillment.

Joan: When I was first married, I admired my husband's stability and calmness. Alan seemed unflappable, which was new to me in a man, since my dad had been an alcoholic.

I was a flexible person and we agreed on almost everything. His first marriage ended because his wife always challenged his preferences. This was never a problem with us, but in another way, I guess you could say it was.

Alan preferred that I forget my parents' problems. I couldn't see why he didn't understand that I had to do something for them. Then the kids came along. They meant more problems and less time. I became the one who had to figure out how to deal with everything while he retreated. I didn't think much of this attitude, and I let him know it. This was supposed to be a partnership. I got counseling and learned to speak up. He learned to play golf, but he wasn't interested in counseling.

Ken: Amanda was really involved in the town where we used to live. I guess I was a little egotistical to think she'd follow me anywhere, as the saying goes, but isn't that what a marriage is about? Well, she followed me, but I guess she got even. Amanda was always a good-looking woman, even after three kids, but I really didn't expect her to get involved with other guys. I was out there in the business world, knocking myself out so we could live in the right house, with the good cars, best schools for our kids, and she . . .

She could have been more subtle about it. Her affairs just about killed me. Alcohol kept my mind off what was going on. I wasn't ready to concede that I had somehow missed the mark, despite the trappings. We looked good, but we never had much to say to each other about things that mattered. After we went to counseling, we discovered our marriage didn't really have enough glue to hold all the pretty pieces together.

Kathy: How is it that what makes you attractive to your husband before marriage can turn him off after marriage? For a long time I couldn't figure that out. I tell my friends, "Stay attractive to your husbands or you'll lose them!" That's what I'd always heard and it made sense. There is a lot of competition out there, even after you're married. My mom was forever fixing herself up for Dad. It seems to work for her—they've been married thirty years!

Anyway, Jim knew I was a physical person. I was a cheerleader and he was a football player. He seemed real happy about my looks and talked about my great body. After we married, there was no way I was going to become a frumpy housewife. I went to aerobics class. I began running. I sort of got carried away. Looking better than most women made me feel more secure in my marriage. It even got us attention when we went out. But Jim started complaining about my time spent at classes. He said I was being self-centered. I still wonder how he expected me to stay in that shape without work.

Bob: I was born on the other side of the tracks and had to do a lot of bluffing to get where I am without going to college or having a supportive family behind me. I love traveling, meeting people, talking them into what's good for them—and me! Deena is a born homebody and I thought I needed that. She would be a sweet anchor.

We complemented each other at first, but as my career developed, I needed more understanding from her about my being away. She knew I was faithful, so that was never a problem. Later I could have used her help as a hostess occasionally. I also expected some respect for my friends. That's when I got into drinking. And the alcohol set off sirens in her head because alcohol was a problem in her family, and suddenly she couldn't accept me anymore.

Marital Aspects

When a relationship that once offered a secure haven of comfort and warmth becomes a source of deep disappointment and depression, we often turn to blame to treat our hurts. As betrayed spouses, we want it known just how badly the other has misbehaved and just who is responsible for spoiling the beautiful relationship we once shared.

After a while, it becomes clear that our spouses will never say, "You're right, after all." Most likely, both individuals have decided that they speak two different languages. The usual ways of communicating to solve problems don't work anymore. The former lovers have taken up emotional residence on distant planets, and from these remote fortresses, each one is firing recriminations at the other for causing the loss of love. The other person is looked upon as a love thief, someone who cheated and stole away the good life.

One party may cling to wishful thinking, but when a marriage hits bottom, it is clear to at least one spouse that the marriage will never be like it once was. Life holds no guarantee that people will change and grow in tandem. Often when growth occurs, one spouse begins to question "givens" built into the beginning of the marriage. For example:

- "Why do I always have to discipline the kids?"
- "Do I have to be the one who takes care of his parents?"
- "Can't I have any friends she doesn't like?"

Figure 2.1. What Happened?

Perhaps one partner seeks a new horizon and the other panics: "I don't need this; why does she?" In recent years, many people have become involved in the search for self-knowledge and discovery. They have found that exploring their emotional lives has given them answers to old puzzles, and dealing with the past resolves inner conflicts. But when they try to communicate their enthusiasm for disclosure of feelings with their partners, they may encounter resistance: "Why get into psychology?" or "Too much analysis can drive you crazy." The partners may see self-exploration as abandonment or betrayal, the "last straw" in a series of growing differences that are bewilderingly new and beyond their capacity to cope.

COMPATIBILITY DOWNSIDE

Usually, compatibility is a big plus in marriage, but often it can work against communication. If two people share the compatibility of openness, they have a good shot at being able to resolve conflict. People who do not hide their feelings much from others tend not to hide much from themselves. Listening to others speak their minds isn't so scary because they are used to processing their own uncomfortable, as well as comfortable, feelings. They can identify with self-disclosure. They do not have to tune out when emotions rise. They will try to feel the other's feelings as well as hear them.

However, if a couple shares the compatibility of defensiveness, they may appear to live in harmony, but this is only because they aren't really facing reality. Sharing the same defensive pattern, they run for cover when they identify a sticky issue. Ultimately, their union may become a rigid citadel through which cold winds blow, chilling their hearts.

Disaster strikes and distance grows when one partner is moved by desperation to change or to seek the warmth of more openness.

ELEMENTS OF EROSION: FLASH POINTS
OF A MARRIAGE BREAKDOWN

The poet Thomas Campbell may have felt "'Tis distance lends enchantment to the view," but in relationships, moments of feeling distant from your love are not the enchantment you had hoped to have in your marriage. Often they are the telltale signs that your spouse is a different kind of person from the one you bargained for. Sometimes it takes a string of these events to realize that they were turning points. You were being compelled by them to see the marriage in a new way. At these times, both individuals often could feel that something was wrong, but the threat was so great that the incidents were not given the significance they achieved in hindsight.

These moments do not usually spring out of thin air or come as the result of unusual major traumas, but occur instead during life changes we all experience. These changes are often ordinary stressful events. How we respond to them highlights our emotional strengths or weaknesses. Attitudes we may have concealed, either intentionally or unintentionally, are in full view and must be dealt with by our partners. If we are in sync and understanding prevails, we weather change together. If our response is too foreign to the value system or response level of our partners, alarms go off.

Some of the stressful events that may send up smoke signals occur when:

1. Either spouse starts a college program.
2. A new job is begun.
3. A move to a new city is necessary.
4. A child is born.
5. A parent dies.
6. A one-career family expands to two careers, or a two-career family shrinks to one career.
7. One or both partners retire.
8. A child becomes seriously ill.
9. Children graduate from grade school to high school to college.
10. Children leave home.

Three more pivotal points, less specific and often quite subtle, can spark deep-seated differences:

1. When unshared interests draw the couple apart
2. When one partner loses respect for the other
3. When one spouse begins to conceal feelings

A "COUPLESHIP"

Of course, many more situations can reveal hidden or dormant attitudes and lead to shifts in relationships. As easily as they can separate people, these events also offer the opportunity for couples to draw closer together, but only if their channels of communication are wide open. The ability to communicate offers the possibility of negotiating different responses than those that can destroy a "coupleship."

When two people seem to grow apart in love, it's usually only one who is growing.

Several years ago I developed a couple's program that continues today as a five-day event. It offers couples an opportunity to explore the dynamics of their relationship. A term grew out of these experiences: *coupleship.* I define it as a passionate, spiritual, emotional/sexual commitment between two people that nurtures both of them and maintains a high regard for the value of each person.

Anyone can have a one-sided relationship with another person, place, substance, or event. It is a dynamic process of a person relating to a parent, friend, pet, possession, or job. As such, it is a one-sided attachment.

A coupleship, however, is two people choosing to have a relationship with each other and the investment in building and strengthening that union.

PARTNERSHIP ALERTNESS

Alertness to what might be significant in the life of your partner is another factor that keeps relationships from sliding into hopelessness. In our busy and active lives, it is easy just to focus on what bothers us and forget that other people might react differently to events we take for granted. A relationship can erode slowly but steadily through neglect so that all it takes is one pivot point to spin it out of control.

TRAUMA: THE POINT OF UNLIKELY RETURN

More obvious direct hits to a troubled marriage are the major traumatic events that may affect one or both partners. These events cause relationship damage that seems too great to heal. Examples of this type of trauma might be:

1. Exposure of a partner's affair
2. Death of a child
3. Bankruptcy
4. Betrayal
5. Mismanagement of money
6. Serious or chronic health issues
7. Preoccupation with child rearing
8. Overextending oneself professionally (workaholism)

Usually when a traumatic event occurs, it has been preceded by a history of problems that needed only one torpedo to finish sinking the matrimonial ship. In a partnership where there is commitment—together with the willingness to face anger, hurt, grief, and vulnerability—trauma has less chance of doing irreparable damage. Trauma can actually bring a couple closer together as they find comfort in each other and mount a joint effort to find solutions to ease the pain.

GROWING CLOSER

Commonality is the glue that sticks people together who stay together. They are committed to creating common friends, a joint home, common hobbies, and sometimes raising children together. The couple has a common future, and within their vision they continue to define themselves as a couple. Those around them think of them together as a twosome, not as individuals with shadowy spouses in the background. These people are together not because they do not want to be alone but because they want to enhance their life by sharing it with this person.

Good relationships involve two factors: what is happening between a couple as two people, and how they, both as individuals and as a couple, relate to the world around them.

In the words of Virginia Satir: "Peace and harmony will come when people pay attention to peace within (individuals), peace between (couples) and peace among (families)."

GROWING APART

Often before anyone notices from outside the marriage, when a coupleship begins to erode or disintegrate, already significant distance-building has been happening inside. Each person, consciously or unconsciously, is beginning to develop more "singleship" than "coupleship." A transition is taking place. Even though a couple may live in the same house, share a sexual relationship and a family, their personal lives are being steered much more toward separate orbits. The marriage itself is becoming an empty house.

Well-cemented relationships contain two people who are consistently and constantly involved in emotional home maintenance. They are attentive to what they are each becoming and how they are interacting with others.

Sometimes singleness creeps up on a person who is basically unaware that major change has begun. Singleness may not even be a conscious thought. We may even hide it from ourselves. Gradually, though, we begin to feel more comfortable by ourselves, thinking on our own, acting on our behalf, making decisions that exclude our partners, and doing things by ourselves that we had once done in our couple world. Now the couple world does not seem to fit right. This shift from a two-some to a onesome seldom is a simultaneous move by either party, although a divorce often looks, from the outside, as though it were mutually agreed upon from the start. The process of becoming single is usually started by one partner who imagines a far better life with someone else or who has felt pushed to the brink by a relationship that has become too painful to endure.

Figure 2.2. Wall

EMOTIONAL DIVORCE

Before a relationship reaches the point where someone mentions divorce, the couple may already have experienced emotional divorce.

Their feelings and behaviors indicate that a definite separation has already happened, even though no one wants to admit it.

An emotional divorce has several warning signs, some fairly obvious and some quite subtle.

Obvious Warning Signs

1. More time is spent with individual friends than with each other.
2. Increasingly more satisfaction is found in work than with each other. Good times with friends and satisfying work and hobbies are important, but excessive attention to these harms relationships.
3. Arguments persist and become more invasive about parents or children. There is an inability to compromise or change behavior.
4. One or both partners are developing a growing dependency on a substance that interferes with health and the ability to feel. These substances include alcohol, drugs, nicotine, and food.
5. One or both partners are developing habits that drain energy from the coupleship. These frequently are gambling or excessive TV watching.

Subtle Warning Signs

Less specific are the day-to-day changes we tend not to notice until coupleship damage is done:

1. Habitual sadness and low energy
2. Boredom and emptiness
3. Indifference to each other's problems and dreams
4. Routine and superficial communication
5. Discomfort with healthy anger
6. Habitual avoidance

7. Decreasing confrontation
8. Sexual coldness/avoidance
9. Loss of capacity to play and laugh with each other
10. Frequent feelings of being misunderstood
11. Frequent feelings of loneliness
12. Overbusy and chaotic social or professional life

Figure 2.3. Problems

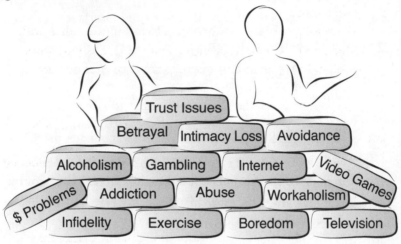

Even more uncomfortable is the atmosphere of the violence of silence in the home: a chill that sends sparks through every room when the two are together. There is a climate of mutual distrust that can transform the former sanctuary of home into an armed camp. Insults and sarcasm may be common, as well as the loss of small courtesies and politeness.

Readiness for divorce or singlehood happens when one or both parties have defined themselves quite independently of each other. Being partners is no longer a major source of identity. Identity now comes from the ways they have chosen to be apart.

At this point in the relationship, when no legal steps have yet been taken and whether or not threats of leaving have been made, there may still be a sense that perhaps some magical solution will descend and prevent what seems inevitable. Since each spouse is operating with a different set of ideas and a different set of rules about the relationship, each finds it hard to believe that the other will not come around to the "obvious" truth about who is to blame and make behavior alterations that will somehow permit the seriously scarred marriage to survive.

THE DISSATISFIED PARTNER

There comes a point when one partner begins to move toward singleness, almost imperceptibly. Perhaps this person is the more contemplative, more thoughtful spouse. We will call this person the dissatisfied partner for the time being. Eventually this person initiates the divorce.

If you identify with this person, you may have spent a great deal of time reflecting and keeping thoughts to yourself. Your concealment is not like lying; it is more like reserving certain thoughts and feelings to yourself for introspection. It is like having a secret place where you can contemplate your situation in private. You may drop the idea of singleness for a while and return to being part of a couple because your thoughts about being single frighten you.

Concern over the apparent approach of singlehood often compels a partner to suggest that maybe the couple should take a vacation, go to a counselor, or sit down to try a different way of talking. The message about the extent of the problem may not be clear to the other spouse. More likely, fear is being manifested as hints. Sometimes a number of little side comments begin as daily complaints. Examples might be:

- "Don't you want to dress up today?"
- "I wish you'd call me when you don't come home."
- "You're not as much fun to be with."

Complaining is an indirect way of saying, "Hey, I'm not really satisfied with us together anymore." Even though it may appear to be negative, it is an indirect attempt to save the relationship, make things as they were originally perceived to be, and get involved in the spouse's emotions in a personal way. A positive response to negative remarks may become the only hope that the partner will rejuvenate as a more interesting, attractive, and attentive person. Unfortunately, it usually rebounds. Very often the unsatisfactory partner will begin to view the dissatisfied partner as a "bitch," "complainer," "nag," or "criticizer." It is hard for the criticized party to see the positive side of the negative remarks: that the complainer is so desperate to make the spouse attractive again, all subtlety has been abandoned and the likelihood of being negatively perceived has to be risked.

Overt criticism may become a last-ditch effort to try impressing a partner with your dire needs, but this approach has inherent difficulties. No one wants to be criticized, challenged, or considered wrong. The inevitable lack of response to blunt personal censure serves only to deepen the disappointment of the dissatisfied partner whose reaction must be to pull even further out of the relationship. This person begins to feel more and more isolated, ignored, and frustrated. Even if requests for the partner to change have been subtle, dissatisfied partners are disappointed that the spouse hasn't reached out to them. They are cast into an uncomfortable limbo, no longer feeling a part of a coupleship and yet not being single. They cannot access the rewards or reinforcement of being a single person but are developing a hunger for validation as an individual now that their identification as part of a team has crumbled. Getting validation becomes very important.

CREATING A NEW IDENTITY

To pursue the security of a new identity, we have to leave our troubled relationships a bit more directly. Generally we try to create a necessary, legitimate absence, such as having to become very, very busy.

I remember at one point in a troubled marriage I became proud that I had three months on my calendar when I was involved in something every single night. I needed the validation that busyness gave me as a person much in demand, wanted, and important. Other people may have thought that my life looked crazily overscheduled as I flew from one thing to another, but for me, and many others, this level of involvement outside the home is enough for a while to make us feel wanted. Joining more groups or finding more activities with friends promotes validation. Support groups, luncheon dates, or friends who frequently go to movies help us prove that we are capable of creating an entirely new social life on our own.

Others simply go back to school. They start taking classes, focus on a new career, or aim for a graduate degree. It is not just coincidence that so many people develop an interest in furthering their education later on in life. They might become involved in some kind of self-improvement course, join a fitness center, or start running— miles from home. A preoccupation with redesigning their bodies parallels the change they hope will occur in their personal lives.

Others prefer to become totally lost in parenting. They begin to involve themselves intensely with one or more of their children. The downside of this is that many times they look to a child to be a surrogate spouse. Later on, when the parents are in a position to form responsible adult relationships, these children feel rejected. Too often children are used to fulfill many of the needs of their parents that should be placed elsewhere.

THE FINAL STEPS TO DIVORCE

Some dissatisfied partners simply "drop out." I remember a friend telling me about her husband who later left their relationship. For about six months before he left, he would sit in a rocking chair in front of the stereo, listening to the song "To Dream the Impossible Dream." He talked to no one, didn't share any particular needs or hopes with anyone, and then one Easter Sunday morning, he stood up from his chair, said good-bye to his family, and walked out, never to return.

Other variations of escape into near-singlehood are developed by those who become very intensely involved with soap operas, football games, or golf. These are solo activities that physically take someone away from a relationship, further isolating them from emotional contact.

The most overt action to render a relationship impossible is that of taking another lover. Unless heroic efforts are later made to save the marriage, the spouse who decides to have an affair will most likely be the one to leave a coupleship by asking for the divorce.

Not every dissatisfied spouse sets out to get a divorce. Most of the time, the unhappy partner is simply trying to find some relief from loneliness in a relationship. As discontented partners begin to collect a positive new identity, they are pulled further and further out of the coupleship. After attempts fail to elicit more positive regard from the partner who will be left, the leaver's need for validation continues to grow. The drive to complete the process becomes overwhelming, and at that point the divorce word surfaces. Frequently the dissatisfied partner becomes so tired of trying to hold up both ends of the relationship with no return that the negatives of divorce no longer outweigh the perceived positives. The end must be signaled, either through direct confrontation ("I'm leaving!") or through intimations by the leaver that the relationship is in really serious trouble and that only one solution is left: divorce.

TRYING TO MAKE IT WORK—TOO LATE

Sometimes couples belatedly go into a period of time called "trying to make it work." Generally it is the person to be "left behind" who holds the most hope to successfully patch up the marriage. By the time a major crisis in the relationship is underway, the potential leaver has already gone through the intense feeling, thinking, and trying processes that the other partner may be just beginning to grapple with. As a result, the dissatisfied spouse probably has concluded there isn't much of a chance. By the time the partner is made aware of the nearness of the marriage's dissolution, it is often too late.

Yet both people may be afraid, for their own futures as well as those of any children involved. "What are my chances of finding anyone better?" "I'm too tired to go back into the dating scene." "The competition is rugged now that I'm older." They may make every possible effort to hang on to the relationship, even though there is no substance left. The known is familiar, despite the fact that it may be awful. An epic effort to make married life "wonderful" may be initiated on the part of the partner who is afraid of being left. Seldom does it feel real, and seldom does it work, because in the real world, the relationship has ended. What worked for them in the beginning no longer exists or was insufficient to carry them through the adversities of married life. The hurts may run too deep.

By this time, most couples agree to go into counseling, but with two very different points of view. One person is going in to save the marriage. But often the other is hoping that the counselor will convince his or her partner that the marriage cannot be salvaged.

Usually a counselor can tell quickly whether there is a chance for compromise and healing. Often the best that can be done—and is considerably helpful in view of the hurdles often ahead—is to relieve the tension, validate each party's right to their own special needs, and reduce the desire for blaming so they are able to deal more directly with each another.

This late-stage counseling shouldn't be confused with the kind of marriage and family counseling that should have taken place when misery first set in. When counseling is sought as a last resort, as leavers are heading out the door, the time needed for rebuilding a relationship isn't available; leavers usually are anxious to pursue the growing security of the new self-image they have been privately creating. The former sense of security from the marriage is gone. They are fearful of opening old wounds.

Although late-stage counseling may be futile in terms of mending the marriage, it can be valuable to help separating couples communicate honestly, minimizing sarcasm or ridicule. While this directness also can cause hurt and pain in the short run, its focus away from changing and punishing the other person is a valuable aid in resolving the division of a household peacefully.

SHARING THE UNIVERSAL FEELINGS OF DIVORCE

We may not know exactly when a relationship begins to grow apart. Perhaps it began as the result of a single event; maybe it was a slow-growing process formed of several incompatibilities. What we do know is that a growing distance occurs that

> *Divorce often is simply the result of seeking validation outside a marriage in which the desired level of approval has become increasingly unavailable.*

destroys the bond between two people, and long before the seriousness of the problem is recognized, the dynamics of separation have begun. Despite attempts to make it work, the marriage falters and one or both of the spouses begin to feel more single than coupled.

The reality of divorce can be shattering and painful and, at the same time, relieving and hopeful. We can all see ourselves somewhere in this book. Although each person's situation is unique, we share certain universal experiences in divorce. It's nice to know none of us is really alone.

Some very frightened people refuse to even think the divorce word. Now that you've read this far, it shows you've got the courage it takes to continue exploring the pros and cons of getting a divorce. Congratulations!

3

TECHNOLOGY AND RELATIONSHIPS

$\mathcal{O}$ ne would ask, "Why is there a chapter on technology in a divorce book?" **Answer:** Desktops, laptops, iPads, and other mobile devices have become part of our daily lives. In some cases, devices have become our most trusted allies. Some cannot imagine being without a phone or connecting device at all times. Always being available by phone often creates intimacy problems for a couple. The one who is on the phone often leaves the emotional connection with his or her partner to form a new connection with the caller. Time away from the phone is necessary for intimate conversations to take place.

All of us have heard the saying, "Well, there is good news and there is bad news." The latest application for that saying is quite likely, technology. We would be remiss if we failed to mention that technology and the whole revolution of communication that technology has afforded us are staggering in importance. Banking, medical research, travel, the ease and access of information, work tools, and education have all been changed quite dramatically with all that is now available to us through technology.

Work efficiency, record keeping, communication, and shopping have all improved in recent years. As a former business owner and longtime author, I find it difficult to recall what it was like to run my business or write prior to having the tools we have come to rely so heavily on today. These tools have made everything so much easier. Younger generations will never know what it was like to cut and paste by hand, or work with a bookkeeper who was forced to use an adding machine, ledger, and pencil.

This is the "good news." My awe and appreciation runs high. However, as I watch our culture and the worlds I am in contact with, I see some of the "bad news." I overheard a mom talking to her eleven-year-old son this week when she said to him, "When you want to say something to me, please come into the room and look me in the eye and say it. Please do not text me from your bedroom."

Dave and Jan were at the restaurant the other night. We sat two tables away. Dave was on the phone while eating, and Jan was reading her iPad.

Diane was eager to visit her granddaughter who lived in another city. Upon her return, she reported that other than one day when they had lunch together and did a little shopping (Grandma buying her granddaughter a new pair of jeans), the granddaughter was on the phone and texting steadily the entire four-day visit. Diane came home with a heavy heart.

Paul retired three years ago and eagerly looked forward to his wife retiring last year so they could do many of the things they had planned for and looked forward to experiencing. Paul has been depressed this year because he cannot get his wife to leave the Internet and her texting. He is even lonelier than when she was working.

In each of the above examples, there was a missed opportunity for connection, sharing thoughts and feelings, and intimacy. Each person remained in her own personal world, using the device that took precedence in the relationship.

What is troubling is that the Internet and electronic technology has provided fuel to the fire that keeps people isolated. While technology provides important additions to our lives in many ways, those who are shy and those who have social problems are able to hide with their devices and avoid personal face-to-face contact and connection with other human beings.

As an author, I am interested in all the ways technology can assist me in my writing. Recently, I attended a conference on the subject.

About 25,000 people were in attendance. In recent years, one of my frequent roles was as a public speaker at conferences. The conferences and workshops in my field were full of energy, excitement, social events, and connections. This computer conference, however, was very different. The people were disconnected. Each one was attached to a laptop, iPad, or mobile phone. The speakers would speak and each person would take notes and then went their separate ways when the workshop ended. The learning part was very helpful and useful, but true connection was lacking. Granted, the goal of the conference was to learn about iPads, social networks, and mobile devices. Yet much could be added to the effectiveness of these devices by addressing the skills, feelings, and creativity that each individual user brings to them.

Where is all the knowledge we lost with information?

T. S. ELLIOT

All of us live in a time when more and more automated systems provide us access to almost unlimited amounts of information. Various websites, blogs, search engines, virtual shopping, and social networking are available to us at the touch of a key. How do we filter through all this raw data that we are exposed to just to find what is useful and relevant to us? Which devices do we want to use, what information matters, and how do we translate this to our personal lives and relationships? It depends on the source of the information, who is searching for it, and how it will ultimately affect that person and his or her personal relationships, whether positively or negatively. This is when technology can begin to influence individuals and families.

It is as though the users of technical devices are architects building their personal lives while connecting with others through relationships. Everyone can use the technology available to enhance their lives and add something to each of their relationships; however, the danger always exists of becoming so attached to their devices that the devices become more important than the quality of their personal relationships.

While it is useful to gather all the information and data that the Internet can provide, the system does lack human interaction. Sometimes we are best served by testing and sharing raw data with family, friends, fellow workers, students, and the general public.

> The saddest aspect of life right now
> is that science gathers knowledge faster
> than society gathers wisdom.
>
> ISAAC ASIMOV

What I want to share in this chapter are the ways we can recognize how we may lose some things to technology and how we can reclaim what we have lost so we can then celebrate how technology works for us.

Relationships and Technology: Is Romance Suffering?

In a counseling session, Kim has shared that she is thinking about leaving her husband because he spend hours on the Internet and it's taking away from many of the activities and shared time together that they used to enjoy. She reports that her loneliest time is when she goes to bed at night. She needs to get the kids off to school and then go to work, so she needs sleep. Her husband reports he needs less sleep and chooses to stay up at night, spending hours on

Facebook and playing video games. Kim is lonely. She feels outside her husband's life and wants to leave to find some companionship and connection.

Mark and Jan used to play cards and board games in the evening, spend their day off on Saturdays shopping for antiques, catching a new movie, or going on a hike. Little by little things have changed. More and more evenings are spent on Facebook and e-mail. Saturdays, when house chores are finished, Jan spends a few hours on the Internet and then texts her friends. Mark would like to spend more time with Jan and feels lonely. Mark rarely speaks of his hurt and anger, but he has started working out at the gym on Saturdays. He has met someone at the gym who also likes to run. They often meet and run together. Sometimes, they go to Starbucks for coffee. The gulf between Jan and Mark is growing. Jan's interests are her mobile devices. Mark is floundering. This is a recipe for disaster that is being played out in many relationships today.

Facebook presents a great deal of relationship problems. It can undermine even the best of relationships. *The Guardian* (February 4, 2012) reported that Facebook is a leading cause of relationship trouble, with American lawyers now demanding to see their clients' Facebook pages as a matter of course before the start of proceedings.

"We're coming across it more and more. One spouse connects online with someone they knew from school. The person is emotionally available and they start communicating through Facebook," said Dr. Steven Kimmons, a clinical psychologist and marriage counselor at Loyola University Medical Center near Chicago.

A 2010 survey by the American Academy of Matrimonial Lawyers (AAML) found that four out of five lawyers reported an increasing number of divorce cases citing evidence derived from social networking sites in the past five years, with Facebook being the market leader. As more and more people spend extended periods of time on Facebook, Twitter, Myspace, and other social networks, they often have much less face-to-face contact. A woman once said to me, "I am so tired of talking to a forehead," referring to conversations with her husband. She also said the same thing in regard to her children.

> [Facebook] levels the playing field of
> friendship stratification. In the real world,
> you have very close friends and then there are those
> you just say "Hi" to when you pass them on the street.
>
> JASON KAUFMAN, RESEARCH SCIENCE FELLOW
> AT HARVARD UNIVERSITY

Family Life and Technology: Is It Fracturing?

No one can deny the help that cell phones and texting have given children and parents in terms of planning, safety, and connection. Many lives have been enriched and possibly saved by these devices.

Yet our price paid in the fracturing of relationships must also be addressed, as was reported by Gary Small, MD, "Laptops, PDAs, iPods, smart phones, and other technological gadgets seem to be taking over pockets and purses, with no end in sight. But could they be altering our families and affecting the way we interact with each other? Investigators at the University of Minnesota found that traditional family meals have a positive impact on adolescent behavior.

"In a 2006 survey of nearly 100,000 teenagers across twenty-five states, a higher frequency of family dinners was associated with more positive values and a greater commitment to learning. Adolescents from homes having few family dinners were more likely to exhibit high risk behaviors, including substance abuse, sexual activity, suicide attempts, violence, and academic problems."

Small continues, "Now, dinnertime tends to be a much more harried affair. With e-mailing, video chatting, and TVs blaring, there is little time set aside for family discussion and reflection of the day's events. Many family members tend to eat quickly and run back to their own computer, video game, cell phone, or other digital activity."[1]

A concern that is often raised in family life is whether or not excessive use of technology is creating a generation of passive people, both young and old. Screen dependency is very real, and screen time (regardless of which screen one is referring to) is a passive process that fails to engage our minds and encourages a type of laziness that inhibits one's interest in activity and action. It quite likely has a great deal to do with our culture's struggle with obesity. I will discuss Internet addiction, which is one type of screen dependency, later in this chapter.

There is a trend in home design that is moving away from the open living areas—where families have the opportunity to come together and share common experiences—into smaller, more separated spaces that offer family members their own tech space, further encouraging separation in the household.

Many child-development experts suggest that all too often children and youth have lost or are losing the ability to entertain themselves creatively. They are developing a shortened attention span. This syndrome is also a problem for the adult population. When the person leaves screen time, they become vulnerable to anxiety in much the same way that those with other dependencies suffer when depriving themselves of whatever vice they use to medicate themselves.

Technology is just a tool. In terms of getting the kids
working together and motivating them,
the teacher is the most important.

BILL GATES

Technology and Friendship

There is so much to say about social networking. At a recent tech conference in Austin, Texas, a panel of academics and social media experts studied the effects of technology on our personal relationships. A question was raised about how many "friendships" we could actually maintain. Also discussed was the meaning of friendship today. Are friendships people we connect with through devices and technology, or are they flesh-and-blood people with whom we talk to, look at, laugh with, cry with, and touch? A text message or a Facebook contact is just that, a contact. You might have 1,000 Facebook friends, but according to Robin Dunbar, a professor of evolutionary anthropology at Oxford University, human brains can really handle only about 150 friendships.[2]

We miss so much when we have too little human face-to-face and personal interaction. Friendships flourish in real-time, person-to-person contact. Device connection does not replace a hug. While information can go between people in a number of devices, an emotional and tactile connection is made when a hug is exchanged. Hugs and face-to-face connections are a vital part of all relationships.

While talking to a group of people who regularly meet for lunch, it was brought to my attention that a need has developed, requiring one to ask that others not answer their cell phones or text during lunch. Some could not comply with this request, and the group disbanded. Those who could turn off their devices continued to meet regularly and those who could not created a second group. This issue reminded me of the smoking and nonsmoking areas in restaurants before most went smoke free.

Every time somebody tries to go in and reinvent what we do, it always ends up being more about technology and sets, and flash and dash, forgetting the main thing, which is interesting people saying interesting and important things.

DIANE SAWYER

Internet Dependency

We now hear phrases like Internet addiction and screen dependency in daily conversation. Yet we do not have a clear and definitive description of what they mean. So far, much of the research consists of surveys, hypotheses, or is anecdotal. Do some people have problems with spending too much time online? Of course they do. Just like people often have trouble with too much eating, spending, drinking, exercising, and more.

Is it an addiction, a compulsive behavior, or a habit? Until we have a clear and proven understanding of cause and effect, what we are left with is the development of mindful, healthy choices as we navigate the world of technology.

It has become appallingly obvious that
our technology has exceeded our humanity.

ALBERT EINSTEIN

THOUGHTS TO PONDER REGARDING
TECHNOLOGY AND RELATIONSHIPS

- Make a mindful decision about how much time you want to spend in front of a screen.
- Discuss your tech time with your family and friends, and hear what they see and feel.
- Consider having a tech room in your home, where everyone works on their devices but can still be together even when they have screen time.
- Eat meals together and do not text, answer phone messages, or have the television on as the focal point of the meal. Share your day with each other.
- Go to bed together with your partner, and eliminate devices in the room with you.
- Do not use tech devices for babysitting and child care.
- It's hard to get a family of varied ages and needs together. Sometimes decisions need to be made and schedules might need to be changed to allow time together. Walk this slippery slope carefully and try to meet each person's needs as much as possible. Make every minute count when you are together. Find some time together without screens. Maybe you can't have dinner together every night, but you can twice a week, without devices, of course.
- Find some board games and projects the whole family can do together.
- Find some television shows to watch together two or three times a week.
- Put limits on texting by offering face-to-face contact with one another. In turn, this personal, intimate contact will become important enough that each family member will begin to monitor his or her own use naturally.

Technology is nothing. What's important is that you have a
faith in people, that they're basically good and smart, and if
you give them tools, they'll do wonderful things with them.

STEVE JOBS

To end this chapter, it is important to note that each of us has the possibility of using technology to work for us, our families, and our friends. While it is exciting and challenging, the greatest impact of technology is its ability to help us connect and learn. Those who will be the most successful will likely be those who excel in keeping both their human interactions and their use of technology in balance. May individuals, partners, parents, and children make wise choices in focusing on the way technology can bring energy, respect, and love to all their relationships. Screen time can bring people together as well as detract from connection. That it can bring people together is what counts.

It's very important when divorces take place and children are involved that the parents consider rules and roles in regard to devices. I recently attended a workshop devoted to the family issues that have arisen when parents have different styles and habits in regard to technology. Leaving a child for a weekend with a parent who spends most of the time on the phone, texting, or on the Internet leaves that child alone a great deal of the time. When one parent has boundaries on the use of devices and the other partner has none, it can cause confusion and inappropriate use by the child. Just as parents try to present a united front with children in other areas, the use of devices is one more area in which parents need to agree.

We have entered into a world where the links we have with one another are enormous. The responsibility of how to use those links lies with partners, parents, and families.

4

THE LEAVER AND THE LEFT: BOTH HURTING, BOTH HEALING

Joan: I used to keep a lid on my feelings, especially when the children were involved. Sometimes I wanted to complain about Alan's approach to raising kids, which basically was to let them do what they wanted. I wished he would take us to the lake more often, like we did before the kids were born. But whenever I even began to suggest we might do things differently, he would freeze up and have something to do out in the garage.

Then, after months of holding back, I'd blow up over something. It was usually unrelated to our biggest problems. But he'd turn on me and right away I'd get defensive because I knew I was overreacting. In some ways it was a relief to be arguing over a safe topic like his leaving the newspaper all over the house. At least we were talking and letting off some steam. That way we could both fight over things that didn't matter. But things that did matter were off-limits and getting worse.

Ken: When we first got married, we had a ball. After being college sweethearts, it was like we were playing house. We were the beautiful people, even belonging to the Junior League. I started joining clubs and service organizations for good business contacts. She got involved in volunteer work. We went out mostly with other couples, business friends. Then we started having less time on weekends to ourselves. The kids were born, but Amanda got them a nanny and hardly slowed down at all.

She loved shopping and socializing. I was always proud of her looks and popularity. I felt lucky to have a good household manager and a partner who got involved in the community. But she just didn't seem to be very involved with me as time passed. I guess I was too busy establishing myself and paying the bills to give that the importance it deserved. Getting ahead professionally and socially was very important to us. I began to notice after several years that we hardly ever did anything fun, just the two of us. As I found out later, no wonder we didn't, since she had other male "friends" available. At that point I felt I had to end the marriage before everyone found out.

Kathy: I explained to Jim that I liked to keep active. I told him if he wanted, he could join me. What else was there to say? I wasn't going to quit exercising and feeling good about myself just to sit home and crochet or whatever. One day I came home from my aerobics class and there was a note on the kitchen table. All it said was "Dance away, young lady. I've left."

I was devastated. He filed for divorce. There'd been no talking about it and no advance warning that things were so bad. He wanted to just throw the marriage away without even trying to work on it. I was lost. I didn't know what else to do except go back to Mom and Dad. I felt I was worth nothing. And I did nothing—for a year and a half. It was as if I was a lump with no life.

Bob: Deena really burned me up. She knew I was a go-getter, hardly the kind of guy who sits with his feet propped up, drinking beer in front of the TV all weekend. That was her dad, the kind of guy she said she was trying to avoid marrying. One of the things she liked most about me before we were married was how I could go anywhere and do what needed to be done. But then she started complaining that I was going and doing too much. How do you put the brakes on sales and success?

All I asked was that she come out of herself a bit to say hello to some nice people once in a while. But no. Instead, she started drinking and smoking too much. Then she started to lose control over our oldest son. He got in trouble and we had to take him for counseling. That's when I found out how much trouble our marriage was really in. And I came to the conclusion that I wanted out.

Any unraveling relationship will result in a split that inevitably turns one ex-partner into a "leaver" and the other into the "left," each with separate sorrows, guilt, problems, and challenges. Certain emotional red flags are hoisted over the home when these critical new roles are about to be assumed. These signs represent levels of deterioration that have been allowed, like rust on a piece of machinery no longer functional, to spread destructively through a relationship. Most often this happens because one or both parties have been unable to talk out critical problems, either by themselves or in counseling.

EIGHT SIGNS OF THE UNRAVELING RELATIONSHIP

Perhaps you recognize these eight stand-off situations from your own experience:

1. Arguments tend to erupt unexpectedly. One partner doesn't even know there is a problem until the other's temper is raging.
2. Negative emotions, especially anger, escalate very quickly.
3. There is a pattern of decision making that puts self-interest above the interest of the relationship.
4. Fear and anxiety mount when you know you have to talk something over with your partner.
5. Fighting usually develops when one person is attacking and the other is defending.
6. You both know what will start a fight, what it will be like, how it will end, and how you will feel. As it begins, there is that "Here we go again" feeling.
7. Your lack of confidence grows in being able to solve a relationship problem.
8. More and more you tend to do fun things together less and less.

Being the First to Leave

What can be harder than making the decision to leave a marriage? It involves all our hopes and fears for ourselves (and any children we may have), and often our friends' and relatives' opinions and our relationships with them. It's never a snap decision—although it may be announced quite unexpectedly—but it builds on a series of negative conclusions that become irreversible when our experiences with our partners don't get better. No matter how much we may talk out with others close to us the pros and cons of leaving, usually the cheering section is very small as we take the step to end a marriage. Friends may know the specifics of our discontent, but few people can imagine the level of inner turmoil behind our decision. Broken marriages can be threatening to others who feel a little unsure of their own marriages, and many friends also shrink from having to take sides.

Often leavers need to find new, caring, and understanding people. The impossibility of fully sharing how hard we tried to save our marriages adds to the guilt, fear, and sadness we, as leavers, usually suffer. Added to the despondency of leaving our hopes behind is the fear of being misunderstood, of being judged as selfish, and of losing important relationships with people who feel they can be "loyal" only to the left-behind spouse. Leavers often feel that they should have tried harder, been willing to change more, and been willing to stay, even if they were perpetually unhappy. Leavers may realize how preoccupied they've been with unmet needs and feel remorse, which hampers their recovery from guilt.

LEAVERS TEND TO GAIN TIME, LOSE SUPPORT

Who was dissatisfied the most? Who made the earliest effort to make the marriage work? Often it's the one we call the leaver. Easily, leavers have some advantages. They have disembarked from the emotional merry-go-round, made a decision, and are no longer expending energy in futile battles and patch-up attempts. They've had time to think through all the positives and negatives of what they are leaving and what they are moving toward. While waiting for the moment when they felt ready to announce their decision, they may even have been able to make advantageous arrangements for finances and a new living situation. Time is on their side. They also have the psychological advantage of being in control of the dissolution of the marriage, rather than perceiving themselves as the "abandoned" ones. If there is any power in the divorce, this person initially may have the greater advantage.

Figure 4.1. The Leaver

Even though the leaver has a sense of power in terms of instigating the divorce, often the one left has unrecognized power within. The power of support from family and friends who rush in to sympathize with the abandoned one can serve as a morale builder, which the leaver may not have during the difficult divorce period. The one left can indeed look like "the good guy," a role easily reinforced by friends and family. Although it feels good, such support can actually slow down acceptance and growth in the divorce process.

Your time is limited, so don't waste time living someone
else's life. Don't be trapped by dogma—which is living with
the results of other people's thinking. Don't let the noise of
other's opinions drown out your own inner voice. And most
important, have the courage to follow your heart
and intuition. They somehow already know what you
truly want to become. Everything else is secondary.

STEVE JOBS

Who Really Was the First *Leaver?*

The person who has been left has a set of feelings that are actually
very similar to the earliest feelings of the leaver: a sense of inadequacy, shame, frustration, and anger. The leaver felt these emotions
on discovering that the one left couldn't or wouldn't change to suit
the leaver's needs. That earlier real-
ization was the point at which the
leaver actually felt abandoned or
"left" by the spouse who couldn't
give what the other expected to get
out of the marriage.

*Leavers need support
systems, too. It's often easier
for the "left" party
to find sympathy from
family and old friends.*

So the real difference between "the
abandoner" and "the abandoned" is
that emotionally the sense of their spouse's leaving them came at different times. The leaver's exit was more overtly expressed, a physical
statement paralleling the emotional separation. In actuality, people
who are left may have been saying no to the marriage for a long
time, but in a more passive way, simply by insisting on being who
they were and not being able to conform to the other's very different
needs. The leavers often suffer longer while delaying their decisions.

Because the leaver had much more time to think and plan, the divorce may feel much more abrupt for the person who is left. Many people I have talked to felt their surprise, anger, hurt, and fear were extremely painful because of this suddenness. Leavers often spend months and years hurting before they finally leave. The ones left are motivated to act fast, make decisions quicker, and often feel they must seek professional help to relieve the sudden spiral into acute pain. But their hurting time actually may be shorter because of the shock that motivated them to get this help.

THE ONES LEFT NEED TO MOVE ON

If we are the ones left, we may have daydreamed that the marriage could be magically saved and parting avoided, despite the negative signs. Perhaps the most wrenching feeling when a divorce takes place is that of being left by someone who once desperately wanted to be with us forever and now can't wait to clear out. Whether love was based on just a fantasy that gradually evaporated or whether unforeseen emotional incompatibilities surfaced in crisis, divorce is extremely painful for anyone who clings to the hope that the marriage could have been saved.

Acute pain has the potential of prompting the one left to seek resolutions faster.

The partner who wants the marriage to continue frequently feels trapped and powerless. Often a great deal of conflict continues between the two parties. If the one left does not acknowledge anger toward the leaver for cancelling the marriage, depression (actually the result of anger kept inside) may set in. If we let this type of thinking continue too long, we erode our self-worth. We need to feel our anger, inadequacy, and fear, but we have to acknowledge them as emotions that will pass. They will become obsolete and we will let them go as we shape a new life.

Figure 4.2. The Left

In addition to being angry, the one left often feels inadequate. "What did I do wrong? Why did I receive this treatment? Am I unlovable?" The period immediately following the event of being left is a critical time for the person surprised by divorce, when it's important to reach out for support and help. Asking for this help is not to be confused with rallying support for ourselves by ex-spouse bashing.

If you feel you have been left, you may need to:

1. Share feelings with an objective outside party in order to drain off toxic feelings that can harm yourself or others. This should be a professional person (counselor, clergy, therapy group). Twelve-step programs are good supports for someone in pain but are not an appropriate place to share and explore the most intense personal feelings.

2. Obtain good legal advice so that both partners can work out a fair and just divorce settlement. It is to the advantage of both partners to make a fair settlement and end all emotional and financial ties. With these connections severed, each partner can become more fully single and independent, and heal from the pain of divorce. Too often financial connections keep the pain in progress.

If children are involved, critical and important issues surround child support. Both parents must assure that the safety and support of their children hold first priority. Many books are devoted entirely to the issues of child support and custody. No divorcing parent has ever regretted the time spent on researching this topic. Many who didn't do this have regretted not learning enough on their own.

The old style of ongoing alimony prolongs the self-image or projected image of each divorce partner as still being part of a couple. This financial link also retards the ability of either partner to recover a sense of sufficiency and self-worth.

Former partners—both the leaver and the one left—who are responsible for themselves only, need to become single, independent people. Among the couples I interviewed, those reporting positive experiences with divorce had ended their financial connections on the day of settlement and divorce finalization.

Release from Pain

There is pain and possibility for both the leaver and the one left. The challenge is not to become bogged down with who has the greater hurt, but to acknowledge and address hurt and hope as stages of growth.

When we have invested ourselves in the life of another and allowed that person to become part of our lives, we may feel as though we are losing a part of ourselves when a divorce takes place. Some spouses have described the sensation as losing a physical component, "a hole in the stomach" feeling. In this vulnerable state, we may be convinced that we will never heal. And yet, with time and effort, we do. When we add good support systems and often professional help to our new lives, the time to heal becomes less and the effort easier.

By reminding ourselves of the circumstances of the leaver and the left, we can again reassure ourselves that both have advantages and disadvantages in a divorce. A leaver is not someone who simply sits down one day, decides to end a relationship, makes a plan, and carries it out. Leavers are people who are or have been acutely unhappy. Sometimes in the very beginning they don't even know it is the relationship they are unhappy with. But they try to help the relationship. They make an effort to confront the situation and solve it in their own way. They make many little choices. In order to protect themselves and to give their changed sense of not belonging some validation, they begin to develop some of their singleness. It is only later that what began as a very subtle restlessness manifests as the decision to leave a relationship.

On the other hand, spouses who are left behind may not be aware that they were actually the possessors of a tremendous amount of power during the relationship. They had the power to maintain the status quo by not picking up on the signals of those first motivated to leave, thereby delaying the divorce process. Possibly the ones left didn't catch the emotional drift of their partners because they were preoccupied with many things: the home, children, jobs, or excess family baggage.

We keep a healthier perspective if we remind ourselves that all along in every marriage there are two people, not one: two people with different ways of handling unhappiness. These two people sometimes begin to drift and become more single. Finally, one of them simply puts a spotlight on reality and says, "This is no longer working. I'd like to end the hurt."

Outsiders will never know or understand the whole story behind any couple's divorce. Moral support is easier for them to share than anger.

With the focus on stopping the pain so that two lives may seek more positive experiences, we may find that divorce is a little easier to view objectively. Learning how differently people express themselves, we see how many divorces are blameless situations in which each partner lets go, acknowledging the other's right to change or not to change, to be as she or he is—for better or for worse—regardless of someone else's needs. This is a right we all fought for as toddlers and even as teens. It is one right we can't expect ourselves or anyone else to forfeit as a maturing adult without enduring an unacceptable level of pain. We release each other from any promises made before we knew what the future held, and we permit ourselves to create a new home with a nourishing atmosphere free of coercion and crippling conflict, where we can grow in peace.

5

TRAUMA RECOVERY BEGINS
WITH PLANNED SELF-CARE

Joan: I think Alan's spitefulness over my wanting a divorce affected me a lot at that time, and it's why I gave up so much. I didn't want to be hateful like him. He felt I had misled him and that I wasn't the person I had seemed to be when we first got married. That last part was true: I had changed. I wasn't a playful little dog on a leash, and I wasn't a follower anymore. First, because he had stopped being the kind of leader I wanted to follow, and then I realized we all need to be our own leaders.

Still, I felt guilty that I got married before I was really ready. Marrying Alan was a way for me to leave a bad family scene. He had been my boss at a summer job during high school. That was when my mother was getting into pills to escape her situation with my dad. So I just escaped with Alan.

When we separated, I was too guilty about leaving him to clarify support for me and the kids. He never has contributed to their upbringing. Now I think it's a wonder the court didn't step in and protect us. I was so foolish back then.

Ken: Between my wife's affairs and the divorce, I wasn't looking very good. I tried to cover up by acting as though I just wanted her to be happy, as if that's all I ever wanted. I let her take the car, the house, the place in the country, the TV, the stereo, the yard equipment—the whole nine yards! See who she's leaving? Mr. Good Guy! I gave her the bulk of my assets. I didn't want her badmouthing me afterward. And I didn't want to talk about it in court.

The entire thing was very embarrassing. But I figured I'd made it once, so I could make it again. Of course, I was older. But after a while I realized that I was also a lot lighter. I had unloaded a lot of illusions and excess baggage, just dead weight. It took several months, but my energy level climbed higher than it had been before we split. Money couldn't buy that.

Kathy: We didn't get involved with lawyers. We had been renting an apartment and were together for only two years, so we hadn't bought much. He took his stuff, I took mine, and that was it. The hard part for me was facing myself as a failure. I just couldn't figure out where I had gone wrong. I mean, a lot of women in my classes were doing just what I was doing and they weren't divorcing. I lay around for a long time hating myself, with little energy to do anything, much less aerobics.

At some point I finally lost interest in hating myself. I guess something in me needed to start moving again. I figured the only thing I really knew how to do was be myself, but maybe I could get more involved with others. I volunteered with kids at a hospice. I had a chance to do summer theater. I made some girlfriends, instead of always needing a guy with me to be with other people. My whole life wasn't depending on one person to care for me and it felt good.

Bob: I wanted out and I wanted it over for good, but this wasn't going to be some giveaway. She didn't deserve it. But there was no way we could talk about a settlement without getting angry. I didn't trust her and she didn't trust me. So we both got lawyers and spoke through them. That really worked out for the best. Let them do the squabbling. I'd had enough. I wanted what was mine and I wanted it over and done with. No loose ends.

Being in my own place by myself was strange at first. I bought a bunch of comedians' records and put them on when I came home. I took a fat marking pen and wrote my best qualities in big letters on sheets of paper and pasted them up in every room so I couldn't miss them. I also listened to motivational tapes just to get some upbeat sounds in my head. And then I spent more time with my friends my ex-wife didn't like and introduced my kids to some of my friends' kids.

DIVORCE!

Prior to the culminating events leading to the demise of what once was a loving and happy marriage, we may push the panic button more than once. Bells and sirens sound. The future may look like an enormous void, the present like a scramble of cold legal moves and hot emotions. We may feel alternately numb and then overwhelmed with countless changes and decisions.

We are anxious to settle everything immediately, to erase the blackboard of unhappiness so we can put all that was (and might have been) behind us. We yearn to find a secure new place for ourselves in the world.

In the midst of all our needs—looking for peace, support, security, and hope—we may distract ourselves from self-care action now. A preoccupation either with the past and how it could have been different or with fears for the future is natural at this period in our lives. Too much introspection, however, can become an energy drain. The person who is filled with rage or nostalgia and dwells on being victimized becomes tired through self-neglect. At this place in our lives we need more energy, not less. We can obtain this vitality through many positive self-care practices.

Whole Person Concept

A longtime romantic concept says that you become "more" when you become part of a couple. In the old Barbra Streisand song "People," we see again the strong message: "I was half, now I'm whole."

The corollary is that if I divorce, I become "half" again. All these messages of society affect our emotions when we divorce, but as we recover from the initial trauma of separation, we can see just how negative and misleading these illusions are. One of the reasons couples often run into serious difficulty is that they have looked to the other to provide qualities they have not developed in themselves. A dependence on the spouse results, and when the spouse leaves, or must be left, a hole is where the sense of being "whole" was.

If we come from a painful family background, we may have a

harder time achieving a healthy feeling of wholeness. Our emotions may be tangled with the classic symptoms of a dysfunctional family past, including:

- Self-denial
- Low self-esteem
- Taking on responsibility for the problems of others
- A low level of self-care

Fortunately, many people who were in difficult situations as youngsters are more able to work through adult stumbling blocks. In therapy they can draw on their history of resiliency and strength. Focusing on the positives of our childhoods, in which we were often required to cope on our own, we may recognize that at a very young age, when we had less experience, we were still able to weather a number of daunting storms. Again, focusing on the positive, we can turn our past coping skills into positive tools for living, using them in a healthy way after a divorce.

A level head with a positive attitude in a healthy and strong body is far more receptive to inspiration and new ideas.

A device to raise our awareness of these skills is the Whole Person Concept Wheel, shown in Figure 5.1. With it you can periodically inventory your own personal powers as a reminder to get you going and keep them charged.

SIX POTENTIAL POWERS

When you stare your post-divorce reality in the face, instead of peering at it through a haze of gloom and doom, you might be surprised at the power you have available to yourself, with or without someone else as a partner. Actually, we all have six potential areas of power, each capable of reinforcing our ability to relate to ourselves, one another, our environment, and the world around us. Becoming and remaining aware of these six areas and their interaction helps us keep in balance. Reminding ourselves of this whole person concept can chase off self-doubt in those wavering moments when we're tempted to feel that we are inadequate.

Figure 5.1. The Whole Person Concept Wheel

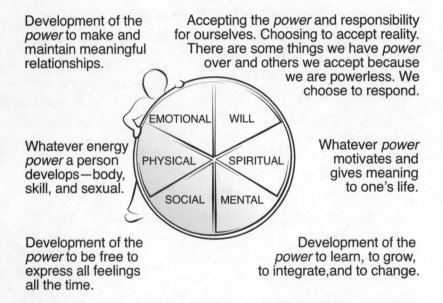

Development of the *power* to make and maintain meaningful relationships.

Accepting the *power* and responsibility for ourselves. Choosing to accept reality. There are some things we have *power* over and others we accept because we are powerless. We choose to respond.

Whatever energy *power* a person develops—body, skill, and sexual.

Whatever *power* motivates and gives meaning to one's life.

Development of the *power* to be free to express all feelings all the time.

Development of the *power* to learn, to grow, to integrate, and to change.

Within every person is a sense of power that is a recognition of the basic fact of our existence. This existence shows ourselves to be what we are. As long as we are physically capable, we are always free to exercise these six powers in expressing ourselves. When we feel robbed of power by circumstances, it is good to get in touch with these essentials:

1. *Our physical power* shows itself in our choice to care for and respect our bodies. Issues of diet, exercise, and grooming are part of this. Ridding our bodies of nicotine and other

harmful substances is an expression we can choose, along
with relinquishing workaholism. Our physical power is a
valuable source of personal energy. It includes our sexuality:
appreciating ourselves as male and female. Making healthy
choices as to how to respond to issues of sexuality is an
important part of our divorce recovery.

This power has more than just a functional use. It can be
employed in enjoyment, such as in sports, music, or touch.

2. *Our mental power* may be directed toward learning,
growing, understanding, and integrating knowledge into
experience. It has three major subdivisions: memory,
vision, and fantasy.

Our memories can help us remember the good times. As
we heal, it will be increasingly possible to reflect on what we
accomplished in this relationship and honor the best parts.
This will be important to our sense of self-appreciation.
Vision is what allows us to look ahead and make plans for
our future. When we can visualize change and consider all
options in our future, we tap into an inner strength and
energy that help those changes come about.

Fantasy is the exciting part. It goes a step beyond vision
and encourages us to imagine and stretch the possibilities.
Many a fantasy became a dream, then a vision, then a plan,
and then an actual happening!

All are beneficial in recovery and should be used for
us rather than against our new needs. We need to use
our mental powers fully in divorce recovery to look at
alternatives, see connections, and set priorities.

3. *Our emotional power* turns us on to the highs and lows,
joys and sorrows, love and hate, cautions and vulnerabilities
of life. It is a source of richness. To feel what we feel, name
it, and talk about it makes our lives more understandable,
less confusing, and less frightening. Our capacity to tune in

to feelings opens us to insight, intuition, and reality. We are capable of experiencing about 150 feelings, and the more we choose to let them come through, the more energy and insight we will have.

Following is a list of many feelings we can use to help understand ourselves and others:

Abandoned	Challenged	Fascinated
Adamant	Charmed	Fearful
Adequate	Cheated	Frantic
Affectionate	Competitive	Frightened
Agonized	Conspicuous	Frustrated
Angry	Deceitful	Glad
Annoyed	Defeated	Good
Anxious	Delighted	Gratified
Ashamed	Deprived	Greedy
Bad	Discontented	Grieved
Beautiful	Distracted	Grounded
Betrayed	Distraught	Guilty
Bitter	Disturbed	Gullible
Bored	Dubious	Happy
Brave	Eager	Hateful
Burdened	Embarrassed	Helpful
Calm	Empty	Homesick
Capable	Excited	Honored
Hurt	Overwhelmed	Shameful
Ignored	Pained	Silly
Impressed	Peaceful	Skeptical
Infatuated	Persecuted	Sorrowful
Inspired	Pitiful	Talkative
Jealous	Pleasant	Terrified
Joyous	Pretty	Trapped
Lazy	Quarrelsome	Uneasy
Lonely	Queasy	Unsettled
Loving	Raging	Violent

Low	Rejected	Vivacious
Lustful	Relieved	Vulnerable
Mad	Remorseful	Weepy
Miserable	Resentful	Wicked
Nervous	Righteous	Worried
Nutty	Sad	Worthless
Obnoxious	Scared	Zany
Outraged	Self-conscious	Zestful

4. *Our social power* is available to affect our relationships with others. When changing a relationship with a significant person in our lives, we can truly appreciate our relationships with all others. We need family, friends, and coworkers to help us through this time. It's a period in which we should use our personal power to meet our needs in many ways. This personal power lets us respond to our needs:

- I want . . .
- I need . . .
- I have . . .
- I'll give . . .

Our social power enables us to offer ourselves to others and to build trust. Knowing when to say no and when to say yes gives us power. We learn to be more assertive in asking for our needs to be met, and also when to say no to a relationship or friendship. As we heal, we choose increasingly healthy connections to the people around us. Social power can be used to develop and maintain close, honest relationships in which we love and are loved.

5. *Our spiritual power* challenges us to find our own values and the meaning of life—how we fit into this world. This power opens us to all possibilities. Choosing to be open to it unites us with others and becomes a thread of connection. Meditation, prayer, and people all become avenues for its

expression in our lives. When a major change or trauma occurs, we are often catapulted into new levels of awareness that include a spiritual dimension. A very wise mentor once said to me, "When you don't know how to go forward but know you can't go backward, you can simply stand still and a transformation will begin." Often this leads to a better understanding of one's spirituality.

6. *Our willpower* is that which decides or doesn't decide, chooses to do or not to do, follows through or changes direction, places values, sticks to decisions, and follows through with promises. This power of volition also has a subtle side: acceptance. Acceptance, when made as a choice, is part of one's responsibility to oneself.

The whole person concept is a growth process, a process of progressively recognizing that you own yourself. It is a way of becoming aware of our own energy and its many facets. It's as if we are becoming the board chairperson in charge of our lives. In this post we would naturally choose as board members only those people who are supportive for us. So it is essential to remember that you are the board chairperson.

As we grow in the awareness of wholeness, we see more clearly our reality as it is. When we choose to be more fully conscious of who we are now, we know we have a right to be this way. We know what a treasure we are, and we know what parts of ourselves we don't treasure enough. Knowledge gives us the ability to choose change.

Developing a Sense of Self-Worth

Another of my books, *Learning to Love Yourself*, talks a great deal about developing a sense of self-worth, the basic ingredient in the motive for self-care. If we take a closer look at the term by dictionary definition, we find that self means a persona or thing having its own identity and personality. Worth is about deserving value and being useful. My own version of the definition is:

Self-worth: *My valuable identity, deserving all good things.*

High self-worth says, "I want to feel high energy and a sense of freedom. I want to know and care about myself." When we're connected with a sense of high self-worth, it means that we are able to . . .

- Make choices that affect the way we live. We are not helpless creatures drifting passively at the mercy of the winds of chance and on the currents of someone else's fortune. We have choices and can actively determine our own existence.
- Enjoy our own bodies. We are multidimensional beings— mentally, spiritually, emotionally, and physically. We can take equal pleasure in all of these dimensions.
- Recognize and accept that the way we feel about ourselves inside affects the way we relate to people in the world. When we feel positive about ourselves, we are able to build and maintain positive, life-enhancing relationships, and we are able to relate to people in meaningful and satisfying ways.
- Truly experience life as we have the capacity to live it. We know that as we raise our own self-worth, we will feel more integrity, honesty, compassion, energy, and love.

All growth depends on a favorable climate, nurturance, and non-hostile environment. Even a tree as big and magnificent as a sequoia can be stunted by harsh environmental conditions. The emotional climate around us is just as influential on our ability to thrive.

Letting relationships just happen to you—rather than purposefully inviting people into your life—is giving up personal power. Surround yourself with those who will support your journey not detour your needs.

You want people around you who are a comfort to you and will help you build strength and confidence. You do not need increased trauma or criticism.

SELF-WORTH PRESCRIPTIONS

Our self-worth continues to increase as we find our lives becoming increasingly manageable. We make it manageable. Life begins to work for us because of the choices we make.

Following are two prescriptions for us and others. One is to enhance our image of ourselves in our own eyes. The next is to help others feel better about themselves through our actions.

Rx for Self

1. Accept yourself.
2. Trust yourself and others.
3. Set realistic expectations.
4. Take risks.
5. Forgive yourself and others.
6. Express your feelings.
7. Appreciate your body.
8. Be respectful of your ideas.
9. Take responsibility for your actions.
10. Affirm your values.
11. Develop new skills.
12. Celebrate your freedom.

Rx for Others

1. Let others know you are listening.
2. Respect other people's right to an opinion.
3. Celebrate other people's achievements.
4. Don't let others guess at your expectations; be clear and reasonable.
5. Enforce rules and guidelines fairly.

6. Appreciate other people's differences.
7. Negotiate conflicts; don't make demands.
8. Demonstrate your trustworthiness.
9. Build confidence by affirming what you want and who you are with others.
10. Encourage other people's independence.
11. Help others with their struggles.
12. Recognize other people's competence.

Our self-worth continues to increase as we find our lives becoming increasingly manageable. The manageability of our lives is in direct connection with the choices we make.

Being Savvy About Legal Moves Isn't Being Mercenary

Parallel with your need to take charge of your emotional health should be a sound interest in the financial aspects of dissolving your partnership with your ex-spouse. So many times a divorcing spouse will become only minimally involved in the legal aspects of the separation, either out of disgust, guilt, or lack of awareness of the importance of being informed; however, most people who took this attitude lived to regret it, not realizing the long-term complications and consequences.

Begin legal self-care with the careful selection of an attorney, one of the single most important decisions that you will make about your future. Find this person through trusted sources: referral by your county bar association or another's recommendation. Switch lawyers if you don't feel comfortable with your first choice.

Like a partner in a business, a partner in a marriage needs to be well represented when the relationship is ending. Don't let strong emotions jeopardize your future; work toward a fair settlement with a competent attorney.

Everyone's settlement is different, according to circumstances, but your goal should be to end the bond in every way possible so each party is free to move on without ties. When children are involved, both partners need to commit to their care and well-being.

LEGAL GUIDELINES

Some guidelines you won't regret following:

1. Freeze all assets for everyone until the divorce is over. Keep only enough for day-to-day living.
2. Avoid the do-it-yourself divorce unless there are no assets and no need for child support.
3. Don't let one attorney represent both parties. It seldom works out.
4. Don't talk directly with your spouse's attorney. Counsels should talk to each other; you talk only with your attorney, who is paid to represent your best interests.
5. Seek firm understanding and good rapport. If you feel you are being asked to do work your attorney is paid to do, speak up. If you feel you are chasing your attorney too often, and unresponsiveness becomes the rule, question the delays.
6. Never lie to your attorney.
7. Act on your attorney's advice. Get what you are paying for.
8. Don't sign any papers or make any agreements without legal counsel.
9. Let your lawyer speak for you in legal matters. If you are inclined to try old manipulative techniques to gain an edge, don't. They may backfire. Unresolved emotions get in the way of making sound legal decisions.
10. Don't take legal advice from friends. Every situation is unique; therefore, you can't safely assume what someone else did will work for you. Laws differ from state to state.
11. Remember that you are the employer and the lawyer works for you. Take responsibility for having a plan, knowing what you want and don't want.

12. Follow through. Do not assume that things will work out by themselves. Pay attention to action. Know what you need to keep track of and do it. Keep your power.

Self-Care Strategies That Work

During the months of loss adjustment, it is beneficial to take the time to focus on self-nurturing, beginning with:

Self-Care Move No. 1: Enjoy the moment. Instead of wondering how others are going to react and worrying about what people expect of you, center on what you're doing that's right for you. Compliment yourself on the matters you handle well; don't let them slide as insignificant. The more you respond to your own needs, the better you will start to feel, and the more positively others will respond to you.

Try to set aside at least one hour per weekday and three to four hours each weekend to do just what you want to do, frivolous or important. Don't do chores. See a movie, watch a fire in a fireplace, read a book, take a painting class, go antique shopping, or go to dinner with friends, but make sure it's what you want to do. This is part of what is called being proactive in your own self-care. You are not waiting for someone else to dress up your life or to serve as its centerpiece. By starting to be creative, you will energize yourself with the results, giving you even more power to rework your life.

Self-Care Move No. 2: Make a pledge that you are going to be more assertive. So much of people's lives, especially during times of trauma, is involved in trying to win approval from other people; however, being self-sacrificing will not help you heal and will not make you happy. Avoiding anticipated external conflict in this way will only result in inner conflict that is just as painful.

Recognize the parts of yourself that are unfulfilled and realize that this is the time of all times to be positive about yourself and assertive about your right to your own life.

Self-Care Move No. 3: Focus on your own needs. A technique that helps many people respond less automatically to requests by others, which may conflict with their own needs and desires, is to pause before responding to any request by children, relatives, friends, or employers. If you have programmed yourself almost always to be "the good guy," the habit of saying yes when you'd rather say no takes a while to break. Instead, try a standard response such as "I need time to think it over" or "I'll have to check my calendar and get back to you." Then take plenty of time to determine if you would say yes because you want to or because someone else wants you to. Make sure the choice is yours. It is very empowering to learn to say no. It will make your yes more meaningful.

Self-Care Move No. 4: Pay attention to financial developments. Take a financial planning seminar, or join an investment club. You need to go only once every week or so, but if you've never been involved in financial planning, it may open up several new horizons. Many said that learning to handle their finances successfully was a major accomplishment following their divorces.

Also, do one financial favor for yourself. Buy a certificate of deposit (CD), look into a mutual fund, buy some stock, and learn how to read the stock report. Each one of these little ventures on your own will reinforce your power to act and will help you feel better about yourself.

Self-Care Move No. 5: Guard your privacy. Don't flee from it; treasure it! Following a divorce many people anticipate intense suffering from loneliness, a negative word that should be turned into a positive like privacy or aloneness. Aloneness is not the same as loneliness. Loneliness is concentrating on who you don't have with you to fill free time. Aloneness is emphasizing the time you have to do anything you want to make yourself feel happy, useful, fulfilled, educated, creative, capable, a part of your community, a positive part of your world, or whatever else you'd like to do to stretch your mental or physical being. Your free time is as valuable as anyone else's. Don't downgrade it because it isn't crowded with demands. Use it to write the letters you've been meaning to write or take the naps you always felt would be self-indulgent. Walk to "nowhere" and back, enjoying every moment and enjoying your "self."

Self-Care Move No. 6: Develop a selection of regular "alone" pleasures. These could be:

1. A special ritual such as reading the newspaper or watching the news with your favorite, or a new, tea or coffee.
2. Getting totally involved in the needs of someone you don't know for two hours a week as a volunteer.
3. Indulging in your favorite dishes at a nice restaurant for breakfast, lunch, or dinner once a week. Find some restaurants where you will feel comfortable reading a book. Savor going out, having a great meal, and enjoying the companionship of a good writer (and yourself!) all at the same time!
4. Exercise—walk, run, swim, bike. You will feel so much better.

ADULT CHILDREN OF DIVORCE NEED SPECIAL SELF-CARE

If you came from a family in which divorce happened, you should watch for the telltale signs of stress reaction after your own separation. You need to be extra aware of what you are doing, when you do it, and why. Children of divorce are often neglected. When they are too young to understand that neglect is not right, children may unconsciously learn and record patterns of neglect as normal and still respond to them as adults. Without realizing that another reaction is more appropriate, you may become self-neglecting after your own divorce.

When Caregiving Becomes Self-Abuse

By needing to help too much—and by helping the wrong people too often—adult children from painful families can set themselves up for abusive one-way relationships. These caregivers have a low sense of self-esteem that may cause them to think they have to settle for manipulators in their lives: addicts, abusers, alcoholics, workaholics, or neglectful friends, children, or partners. But when caregivers decide to change, they become more aware of how they let people treat them. Do they want to continue to permit friends and relatives to take advantage of them, misuse their company, criticize their lives or choices, put them in a position they don't want to be in?

Very often family members will try to make divorcing parents feel guilty by dumping their anger on them rather than taking responsibility for their own feelings. This can become a painful burden to carry.

For adult children of divorce, learning to take care of yourself may be very hard to do. Practice will take you from discomfort to comfort without feeling guilty.

Sometimes a change in behavior—a refusal to continue being a victim of exploitation, regardless of another's apparent need—begins with a simple evaluation of your own needs. Do I need to continue in so much discomfort and pain at this point in my life? Can I survive the trauma of divorce by carrying this additional destructive baggage? The temptation to give in to the old way of holding on to companionship will remain for some time because:

- It is familiar.
- It has become automatic.
- It is easy.
- It feels like part of us.

Choosing to be exploited is like the compulsion to do anything else we know isn't good for us: it feels nice for a little while but bad for very much longer.

It is critical for people who have been overly responsible as children, and have taken this behavior into adulthood, to find relationships at this time that are mutually nurturing and supportive. We all need to associate only with people who respect us. We need to learn to identify with our own needs and surround ourselves with people who support—not work against—what we are trying to achieve in our new experience of being on our own.

People who want to force their ways on you are counterproductive in divorce recovery.

When Self-Care Becomes Self-Abuse

Some of us have grown up in homes where we had to take care of ourselves too much. That became the norm, the main way things happened. Often we were required to reach beyond our grasp, and we "made do" with the results. Whether the outcome was satisfactory or unsatisfactory, we may have turned our unhappiness into a pride that we could do it ourselves. Pride is a good feeling, but too much pride is counterproductive.

You cannot be on someone else's "own" and be on your own, too.

In times of adult crises, such as divorce recovery, we may find that we'd like to bend our tendency to handle every situation by ourselves. We may want to ask for emotional or practical help but are afraid that it could come with strings. Maybe accepting help would feel uncomfortable or threaten our valued sense of independence and control.

Sometimes breaking the patterns of our responses to difficulties can open a new, much more comfortable world for us. Human beings

Healthy behavior can feel unhealthy at first because it is not our norm. Giving and receiving help are both part of healthy living and mutually rewarding.

are social beings, not isolated organisms. Reaching out for emotional or practical support from someone who has not misused us in the past is healthy. Sufficient help may not have been accessible to us as dependent children, but it is readily available in many forms, including professional counseling, now that we are adults. Taking advantage of available support not only puts us in a position to do better faster but gives those who like to help a chance to feel good.

Twenty-One Healing Helpers

You may be surprised by how many ideas are available as quick pick-me-ups, ideal for the recently divorced. That's because we who have been through it have had plenty of time to find out what works. So while you're working on deep issues that will take a little time to sort out, here are twenty-one quick-healing helpers to offset periodic blues:

1. *Swamped with nostalgia?* Instead of sobbing too much over the wonderful times in the beginning and how they went away, turn the emphasis around. Remember how wonderful you were in the beginning—approachable, lovable, and desirable—and how you made the great times happen as much as anyone else.

2. *Feeling unappreciated?* Compliment yourself every day. Maybe your hair turned out great. Or you got a report in on time at the office. Maybe you made that sale. Be generous with self-praise.

3. *Suspect you're not good company?* Negative people are not enjoyable to be around. A simple way to be sought after is to be aware of other people. Give them genuine compliments.

Look for things to like, and people will like to be with you.

4. *Can't imagine your life ahead?* Creative imaging takes time and practice. Give yourself plenty of time to just daydream and try on possibilities. Like a good sauce that needs time to simmer, daydreams can fulfill your heart's desire in time. Let your thoughts roam; you don't have to plan the rest of your life immediately.

5. *Wish you could get what you want?* Start asking. When a new relationship materializes, speak of your needs. Although awkward at first, speaking up gradually becomes very easy. You can begin with something as small as requesting the TV remote. Don't always let someone else make the choices. Even those who like to be in charge appreciate a break. You choose the movie. You pick the restaurant more often. Let people know who you are by what you want.

6. *Feel as if you're just marking time?* Decide to grow a bit. Learn something new. Would you like to play a keyboard? Do you really wish you knew computers? Don't most of us want to be able to speak a little Spanish or French when traveling? Would you like to go to a sneak-preview movie? All of these activities are things you can do by yourself. And they will all give you a sense of mastery over your environment.

7. *Swamped with the mundane?* Learn the principles of "delegate or ignore." Don't define yourself by how much you can endure. Whether doing dishes, cleaning house, grocery shopping, doing your taxes, or arranging reservations for a trip, do what you want to do, then delegate. If it's not important enough for you to do or to delegate, don't add it to your list of woes.

8. *Not laughing enough?* Listen to comedy tapes. Clip some cartoons and hang them where you'll be reminded you can still laugh. If you can't think of anything funny to say, share a cartoon with someone. Try not looking with a microscope

at what went wrong in your day. Imagine you are boarding a plane and then looking down on your day from 30,000 feet above it. A change in perspective can make molehills of mountains, at least long enough to chuckle at some of the things we see in a one-sided way.

9. *Running out of options?* There are always going to be problems in life beyond our control, and yet many things are controllable. Even when they aren't, we still have a choice in how we handle them. When are we going to let something become really big? When are we going to address a problem? When are we going to take action?

10. *Can't think positively?* All of us have the option to think positively, but it may not feel right to deny our negative feelings. So have your cake and eat it, too. If you want to say "I'm too fat," follow the negative with "but I'm starting to exercise" or "I didn't overeat as much as I could have." If you feel "My money's running out," don't pass up the chance to add, "but every single day I'm looking for an opportunity to make more" or "but I'm working on how to manage it better." Celebrate the choices you're making and the critic inside will lose its power as the only influence over your emotions.

> *Affirm every day what is going right in your life, as well as your role in making good things happen. Don't give up your power to a negative pattern of thinking.*

11. *You feel like a lump on a log?* Make exercise fun and social. Walk in malls. Join a spa. Hike. Get a trainer. As you feel good about yourself physically, you will feel better emotionally.

12. *Racing against time?* Give yourself a minimum of a year to restore balance, hope, and positive feelings. You will need to experience each milestone (Thanksgiving, Christmas, Hanukkah, Valentine's Day, Easter, Fourth of July, birthdays,

anniversaries) before the grief cycle is completed and the relief of emotional healing sets in. Time will heal.

13. *Life too hectic?* You may need to create quiet time to reflect, meditate, read . . . an interval to fill with meaning.

14. *Need support?* Contact with understanding people is easily available in support groups, counseling, therapy, or 12-step groups. Seek people with both similar problems and without present difficulties. Each group has something to give what you need.

15. *You can't live in the present?* A sane starting point in divorce recovery is to see things as they are rather than the way they were or as we wish they would be.

16. *You're intimidated by your kids?* You can expect them not to understand an adult's decision, but don't feel guilty that kids may pout as a result. Shift the focus to what they can understand: you love them and they will always be taken care of.

17. *You doubt you can be two parents in one?* It is easy for single parents to become prisoners of their children by trying to overcompensate in every area. Trying to be two people only results in one tired parent. Substitute guilt with more love not more activity.

18. *Do you miss belonging?* Develop a family-of-choice, an emotional safety net. There are many ways to find supportive people in groups you join. If you don't know how to find them, check with your local newspaper to see what day they print notices of support group meetings.

> *If we want to grab hold of a better future, we must let go of the past. Newness needs a space made for it.*

19. ***You can't forgive?*** There are many paths to forgiveness, some very effective ones begin with an understanding of ourselves. Ultimately, when we are able to let go and see a better life ahead, we can let forgiveness become a spiritual experience rather than a thought process.

20. ***You're afraid to remarry?*** Statistics indicate that the majority of all divorced people remarry, despite reservations after their first marriages fell apart. Most people, in time, realize that they are more capable of healthy commitment because of the insights they've gained through the divorce experience. They may meet resistance to the idea of remarriage from relatives or friends, losing some relationships and gaining others. It's sometimes "win a few, lose a few," but the best way to move into a new marriage is to expect bumps that will be smoothed out a day at a time.

21. ***What-ifs troubling you?*** We all make mistakes in marriage, but at some point you may realize that this old saying isn't just a cliché: You are human, too. Making the decision to let go of the "why" questions, the blame, and the guilt will free you to emphasize your strong points and learn from your weaknesses, not dwell on them. Knowing you have a good heart, send it confidently out into the world and watch it confirm what a good person you are.

6
COLLABORATIVE DIVORCE AND MEDIATION

*A*bout half of all marriages in the United States end in divorce, most of which are handled by attorneys and often result in unnecessary collateral damage. Many have come to believe there is a better way. For this reason, I have chosen to devote an entire chapter to learning more about this better way. It is called collaborative divorce, which calls for a team of caring specialists that includes two lawyers, two coaches, a financial consultant, and a child specialist (if children are involved). The goal is addressing the needs of everyone who will be affected by the divorce. It is a new paradigm that empowers the couple (rather than lawyers or judges) to shape the outcome of a divorce.

> You will either step forward into growth
> or you will step back into safety.
>
> ABRAHAM MASLOW

I first heard of this approach when talking to a family member who is a certified public accountant (CPA) and very involved in this type of divorce approach. I liked the idea as presented and began to study more. *Collaborative Divorce—The Revolutionary New Way to Restructure Your Family, Resolve Legal Issues, and Move on with Your Life*[1] is an eye-opening book that offers hope and help when families are facing such an enormous change in their lives. The authors provide a visionary concept and an intelligent contribution to people facing divorce. *Collaborative Divorce* should be assigned reading for every divorcing spouse.

According to authors Tessler and Thompson, the very first collaborative lawyer was Stu Webb, who began this work in Minnesota in January 1990. His idea made such good sense that the news quickly swept across the legal world. By 2000, trained collaborative lawyers could be found in most major cities and many smaller towns across North America. Today, collaborative lawyers are easy to find. Meanwhile, as lawyers were embracing collaborative law, the team approach was also being born. Originating with the work of Peggy Thompson and her peers, the disciplinary team approach was first offered to clients in Northern California in the early '90s. Pauline Tesler and Peggy Thompson continue together and separately to teach collaborative professionals in North America and Europe the skills of interdisciplinary team collaboration.

Some people take the heart out of you
and some put your heart back together again.

UNKNOWN

Much has been written in many states about experiences with this type of divorce approach. It promises to help many families. Steven Rutlen, CPA, in his article "Divorce, It Doesn't Have to Be a War!" wrote: "The traditional legal process of divorce is by its nature adversarial—husbands, wives, and their attorneys working against each other with the ultimate objective of winning the war. Once invested in the battle, the couple relinquishes control over their futures to their attorneys and the courts. Threat of litigation becomes the leverage used by both sides to extract concessions and agreements. If agreements cannot be reached, decisions are conceded to a judge. The divorcing couple often feels a loss of control over themselves and their futures."

Consider Char and Mike. Mike is an engineer and holds a top-notch job. He works hard and earns good money. Char is an artist and loves beautiful things. Mike and Char look like they are very different, but in many ways they share similar backgrounds and interests. They are both from the Midwest, they both love to ski, and they

both enjoy cooking. Even though their careers and personal aspi-
rations are very different, they met on a skiing weekend and were
attracted to the parts of themselves that were similar.

She was intrigued by Mike's career, looked to him as a winner, and
found him to be an exciting man. Char loved the special weekends
he set up for them. He loved her quirky and lighthearted, artistic
ways, and she was a pure delight to his otherwise structured life.
They were married ten months after they met.

For two years they had a wonderful life together. They vacationed
together. Mike continued to work hard and continued to make
enough money to keep their lifestyle fun and exciting. Char created
a greeting card company. Mike invested in her efforts. She had great
fun, but the company made very little money. It was more of a hobby.
She then wanted to go back to school, so Mike worked and Char
took painting lessons. As planned, she became pregnant. Baby one
was a little girl and both parents were delighted.

When the little girl was about eight months, Char decide she was
tired of full-time parenting and painting and now wanted to take
sculpture classes. She talked Mike into a full-time nanny and pursued
her dream to become an artist who specializes in sculpture. Money
was now a little tighter. Char became pregnant a second time. This
time they became parents of a baby boy. For a while, Char became
a full-time mom. Again, in about six months, she was restless. Not
only did she want to go back to having a full-time nanny, she wanted
to go back to school full time, too. She also felt that she needed an
extended vacation and wanted to go on a lengthy cruise.

Mike shared with her that money was getting tighter. The addition
of two children, her request for an extended vacation, wanting to go
back to school full time, and hiring a full-time nanny with only one

salary in the family was too much. Char was enraged. She and Mike began to argue. She held her ground and became even more demanding. Mike was overwhelmed. He loved his children and worried about them being around such an angry mom. The next few months were full of accusations back and forth, rare sexual contact, and blame toward each other. Finally, Char surprised Mike with a petition for divorce.

The process began. It ended with attorneys each fighting for the wishes of each person. Char wanted alimony, as she felt she had given good years of her life to Mike. She wanted four years of college paid for, as she now decided to become a social worker. She wanted a full-time nanny, a paid vacation once a year as she had become accustomed to, support for each child, a full education for each child, medical and dental coverage, and the family home. Mike saw his life unfolding before his eyes with no attention being given to any of his needs. He felt helpless, afraid, and angry.

By the time the divorce was final, Mike had lost most of his savings and was expected to fulfill almost all of Char's demands. Because of his love for his children, he signed the divorce papers. He felt his energy and most of his life's dreams being sucked right out of him. He had no recourse and found himself paying all expenses for Char's demands. It was an unfair decision and a painful outcome.

Hearts will break, but even broken will go on.

UNKNOWN

Emotions were volatile during the divorce process, and Mike conceded on several counts simply to keep Char civil and protect the feelings of the children. In many ways, Mike gave in to "keep the peace." He paid for it the rest of his life. Divorce is a touchy journey. It is easy to feel overwhelmed and easier to do anything to reduce the stress. Sadly, this is also the time people make decisions that affect them in very important ways forever. One needs to recognize that there is a diminished capability to make good choices that are well thought-out. Usually, we like to think of ourselves as thoughtful, fair, reasonable, and intelligent. Yet those strengths during the divorcing time may turn into fears, need to control, lack of energy, and confusion. One just wants the stress and pain to end.

Let's look at David, who is a physician. His life is about helping people and responding to crises with answers and hope. When his wife of twenty-five years had an affair, he was crushed. How could this have happened? He was hurt and embarrassed that she'd slept with a friend of his. He had supported her in style during those years of marriage. He was doubly embarrassed because he was the last to learn of her affair.

Friends had known for some time. He had always thought of himself as a competent and caring person. His image was very important to him. Not only had he somewhat spoiled his wife, he had also spoiled his children. He worked hard as a student, an intern, a resident, and then as a doctor. He felt guilty that he had spent so much time at work and loved it so much. His children had learned to manipulate him through his guilt and demanded much more from him while giving little in return. However, with his wife's affair, he reached a breaking point and eventually filed for divorce. His wife, used to being taken care of, was shocked and amazed that he would not plan to keep her in the style to which she had become accustomed.

In her divorce settlement, she wanted the family home, the insurance policies, inflated alimony, and more. Her children stood by her side and saw her as the injured victim. They had no idea about the affair; David was unwilling to share that part of the situation with them. In fear of her wrath, he was willing to give her everything she wanted. His attorney initially advised him against doing so, but his fear of her disapproval and gaining his children's approval were bigger than common sense. His attorney allowed this unfair and unjust settlement to be made. Since the divorce, David has paid for that decision every single day for the last twenty-five years. A team working collaboratively with him would have supported a fairer outcome of this situation.

Divorce Considerations

Divorce is a time of sorrow and grief for everyone. It also demands that we work through feelings of loss, guilt, and shame. Professionals can help with this process, and the wise person calls upon this help rather than give in to unreasonable demands. It's never easy for anyone, but you need not surrender the rest of your life because you are making the decision to divorce.

It is dangerous to feel that marriage must be the way it has to be. Just because our culture makes marriage the norm doesn't mean that divorce is bad. Many times divorce is the sanest and healthiest avenue a couple can walk. Only in fairy tales do all relationships bring happily ever after. In reality, that sometimes is not the case. False beliefs about marriage always working can be complicated by inaccurate myths that people have about divorce. Friends, family, and the law seem to need to define the good person and the bad person in the marriage instead of looking at the fact that maybe this marriage has reached obstacles that cannot be overcome.

We took a step in the right direction when we were introduced to the no-fault divorce, which has been part of our culture for many years. This is a vast improvement over American film director Woody Allen's observation of New York's divorce law that required proof of infidelity, which, as Allen pointed out, is forbidden by the Ten Commandments.

Even though no-fault divorce is available throughout the United States, it is still a misleading idea. You do not need to convince a judge of some fault your spouse committed in order to qualify for a divorce; however, the courts still are set up to find fault and allocate responsibility. This stance fits and is compatible with the cultural idea that someone needs to be blamed. Shame and guilt still drive the decisions made around divorce. Most divorcing parties are more likely to blame the partner than assume their role in the breakup of a marriage.

Figure 6.1. Divorce Options

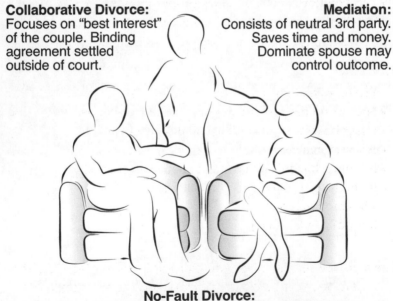

Collaborative Divorce:
Focuses on "best interest" of the couple. Binding agreement settled outside of court.

Mediation:
Consists of neutral 3rd party. Saves time and money. Dominate spouse may control outcome.

No-Fault Divorce:
Contrary to popular belief, courts are set up to find fault. Shame and blame will dictate outcome.

Understanding Collaborative Divorce

People do have choices when it comes to divorce, and a collaborative divorce is one of those options. The strength of this type of divorce lies in the experience required by counsel, and the advice offered comes from multiple perspectives that, if navigated well, will provide the best possible outcome for all parties involved. Collaborative divorce offers the couple information, emotional support, and built-in protection for the children.

Other benefits offered by this type of divorce include:

• Focuses on resolution instead of conflict
• Helps you to find the places you can agree on
• Helps you find clarity
• Points out your shared values
• Helps you face serious differences with a goal of cooperation
• Lets you learn about law and legal positions without threat
• Teaches you how to co-parent and protect the children

Some of the pitfalls to be wary of with a traditional, lawyer-focused divorce are:

• Presumes that divorce is wrong and must have fault
• Focuses on the past and does not plan for the future
• It is primarily about conflict and disagreement
• It is very expensive
• It is often hurtful and favors one person over another
• It doesn't give enough help and clarity
• The emotional cost is high
• It is often unfair to one or the other party

There are no super powers, no extraordinary intelligence. The hero lies in an ordinary person who faces tragedy with courage and soars through the difficulties.

VICTORIA LONGWORTH

Mediation Divorce

Another alternative to traditional divorce with a lawyer is mediation, a settlement meeting where the parties are assisted by a third-party neutral who acts as a go-between. Usually the parties will mediate child custody and financial issues, property distribution, and spousal support. Each person still has a lawyer, and the mediator goes back and forth and tries to work out settlements.

Sometimes mediation is implemented without lawyer involvement. If a lawyer is not present, a mediator will not deal with the legal aspects of the divorce. It is important to know that they are not judges or arbitrators, and they have no power to decide what is best in a case. They are there simply to help the parties settle disputes. Mediation's purpose is to encourage open discussion to help in settlement issues. It is an alternative to formal divorce court. The mediator is an objective person. It is the mediator's job to help the parties clear up disagreements and come to terms they can both agree to.

Why do a mediation? Mostly it is to save time and money. If all goes well, it shortens the divorce process, which is better for the couple and the system. Because mediators are not invested in the outcome, nor do they represent either party, they can often see areas to agree where the invested sides cannot. Mediation allows for more privacy because nothing in mediation is recorded by the court.

What Is the Difference Between Collaborative Divorce and Mediation?

Knowing that lawyers are not the core of either process, people can become confused wondering what the differences are, or if they are both the same.

First, the power distribution is quite different. In mediation without attorneys, the dominant spouse can control the outcome. The role of mediator is not to take sides. If one person has a greater income, he or she may be able to lobby for a greater share of the income. The mediator cannot stand up for the rights of the lesser income party. This party may get run over by a strong, dominant spouse. If one person had an affair, he or she may enter the mediation with so much guilt that he or she chooses to give up everything to deal with their guilt. Because they cannot take sides, mediators are not able to point out what is going on. In the collaborative process, however, each person will have a lawyer, and the lawyers will work together to smooth out imbalances in order to reach a more fair agreement.

Second is the advocacy issue. Divorce is always stressful and painful. People handle both very differently. The collaborative process provides attorneys with the ability not only to assist with the managing of emotions and help keep a workable solution in the forefront but also to provide financial and emotional expertise.

Third, a major difference is the "interest-based negotiation." Even though mediation is based around a lawyerless agreement, it still means there are two sides and the focus is on meeting in the middle. Collaborative divorce focuses on the "best interests" of the couple and tries to meet these positions rather than negotiate hard positions that belong to one or both the parties. It's a subtle difference, but an important one.

For more information, you will find collaborative divorce resources in your local phone book or from any computer search engine.

> Outer changes always begin
> with an inner change of attitude.
>
> ALBERT EINSTEIN

Tips for Healing from Divorce of Any Kind

- Ask for support from only your closest friends and family members. Lay ground rules that you do not want judgments on you or your partner; just to be there for you, and if there are children, maybe offer some help with time commitments. Let them know they are important in your life during this transition time.
- Take care of yourself (body, mind, and soul). Find every ounce of energy and positive thinking you can drum up. Get enough sleep, exercise, and use meditation, yoga, or prayer to center yourself. Watch out for binge eating, too much TV, and sleeping too little or too much.
- Make sure that even during the transition time, you are well covered by health insurance. Getting ill or having large medical bills will only complicate an already confusing and difficult time.
- Refuse to nitpick or banter with your ex-partner or anyone connected to the divorce. Small fights and negative talk will make a hard situation only harder. Take breaks when negotiating, and keep it clear and direct.
- Do not use your ex-partner, family, or friends to vent your bottled up feelings and thoughts. This is the time to see a counselor, join a support group, or talk to a clergy at your church. You can find many inexpensive services, and it will be much better for you than leaning on those closest to you. Never use your young or adult children for this purpose.
- Think long and hard before you put anything in writing. Anything you post could be around forever, and your life may change in many ways. Do not tie yourself down to any current words.
- Exercise, exercise, and exercise some more. You can walk outside absolutely free or do the wonderful tapes of

Leslie Sansone indoors. (Do a Google search to find Leslie
Sansone walking tapes.) Friedrich Hermann Nietzsche
said, "All truly great thoughts are conceived by walking."
- Be careful about rebound relationships. You are in a vulnerable
  state and not processing emotions as clearly as you might
  want to be. Slow down, take your time, and recover all the
  parts of yourself you might have lost in this difficult process.
- Be careful and mindful about spending money. It is all too
  tempting to make yourself feel good with shopping and
  services. Watch your expenditures until you have settled in
  and become used to a new financial picture. Debt will only
  increase stress.
- Listen to yourself and give yourself as much space and time
  you need to feel tranquil, peaceful, and in charge of yourself.
  Make your living space as inviting and cheerful as possible. I
  love the saying "Instead of waiting for someone to send you
  flowers, buy them for yourself." For me, fresh flowers in my
  living space is a must. Put away old sentimental items. Don't
  look at them for a year. Then decide to keep, sell, or give away.
- If you have an animal, be sure it's well cared for. It needs food
  and exercise. They are sensitive to your presence and absence.
  Be sure you are there for them. If the settlement meant you
  might have lost a pet, you may want to think of getting a
  new one.
- Forget about any kind of revenge. It has a way of backfiring
  and coming back to haunt you.
- Don't lose your sense of humor. Bring some lighthearted
  comedy into your life. Rent old movies, go to a comedy show,
  or watch silly sitcoms. After all, laughter has proven to be a
  dependable healer.

In the long run, we shape our lives and we shape ourselves.
The process never ends until we die.
The choices we make are our own responsibility.

ELEANOR ROOSEVELT

7

FEELINGS NEED TO BE FELT

Joan: I was feeling sad, missing what I didn't have, and I was lonely. After the divorce I felt vulnerable. I needed people, as much support as I could get. I went into therapy because I had been over-eating and gaining weight due to my depression. I joined a support group of divorced people and a weight control group, and I made some friends I could talk to. Some of them were women and one was a man.

Maybe I was taking a shortcut out of unhappiness, but I married Doyle. Even if it was a shortcut, I felt more able to take chances and less in need of a fatherly husband. Still, it was a bit much to handle, still recovering from one marriage while taking on a new one. But my therapist was there for me, regardless of what I decided to do, and so were my new friends.

Ken: For some time after the divorce, I was numb. Thinking about the whole thing just hurt too much, so I started drinking too much, which, of course, just prolonged the agony. I felt nothing was chang-ing, except for my new drinking problem. I had to get better, so I made a strong commitment to an AA group. I lost a lot of self-pity there.

I began having social breakfasts and became involved in other people's lives. I was feeling really ineffectual with my own kids, so I decided to get active in some adolescent programs, working with disadvantaged youngsters. That was an upper. Then I figured I might as well stop smoking, as long as I was starting a new phase of my life. I started playing golf for some exercise and went swimming regularly at the Y. After a while, instead of seeing a bleary-eyed guy in my mir-ror, I started to look pretty good.

Kathy: I was a zombie for the longest time. I thought my depres-sion would never end. My mother had to take care of me almost like a child for a year 'cause I really wasn't interested in doing anything.

Thinking just made it worse. I'd trashed my marriage and that was it.

As I came out of it, I started having mood swings. One day I'd feel I was young enough to get another guy, have a career, and make it on my own. Then I'd have a lot of energy and go out running. But the next day I'd crash, wonder what I had that anyone would want; and I'd get really depressed about not being able to hold on to Jim, how great I thought he was, how beautiful the wedding was, how blind I was, and so on.

In counseling I got a better perspective on myself. I had been afraid of feeling regrets for the rest of my life. I saw I had really limited ideas about myself and what I could do. After a while I got up the courage to experiment with my life and try some new things.

Bob: Spending more time with my business buddies and other friends, I began to find out that maybe they weren't a great influence on my kids or even on me. I decided to take my teenage son fishing in a new boat we'd shopped for together. He looked forward to these times and so did I. My daughter seemed to lean on her mother more, but I was there for her, too.

Then I did some things for myself. I dated. I stopped drinking entirely, and two years into the divorce, I was able to stop smoking. Things were rolling again, and better without the constant conflict. I'd recommend to anyone in my spot to put the Serenity Prayer in his wallet. It's realistic and it helped.

Healing Through Grief

Shortcuts don't work with grief. The only way to heal as quickly and as thoroughly as possible from the wrenching grief of divorce is to walk right through the center of it. You can't go over it, under it, or around it without it coming back to haunt you. Why not? Because those feelings are you, and you can't escape yourself.

If we try to bury pain with work or fog it with alcohol or food, recovery is going to take even longer. Those who do not allow themselves grieving time just put off the process. Later in life the pain will boomerang, returning to hit us as a neurosis, a compulsion, or some other kind of self-defeating behavior. At that point we will have double the work to put our lives back on track.

We need to take the time to examine all the emotions that are affecting us, to try to trace them to their source, to see how and why the relationship went wrong, and then to adjust our minds and hearts to the new view of ourselves and our former spouses that will emerge. Grief is part of gaining a new perspective on what was real in our lives—past and present—and what was fantasy. What we grieve over may gradually change in the long reexamination process that is part of the recovery period.

How long will it take? Some people take longer than others, depending on whether they were the leaver or the one left, whether the decision to divorce came suddenly or was brewing for some time, and depending on the nature of the individual.

Fortunately, pain like this doesn't come often in most lives, but this makes it even more unfamiliar and uncomfortable. We want the pain to stop, but it is in our best interests to learn its lessons rather than to try to anesthetize it.

Healing from the grief of divorce will happen. As with other hurts, we heal best and most completely if we let all of our feelings drain from the "wound."

We need to recognize that following divorce, life isn't going to be easy for some time. We need to recognize that it is okay to be frightened of the challenges ahead. It's okay to mourn that the dream we once loved to dream is over. Grief is natural and must be allowed. As we reach out for help and go ahead to do what needs to be done, we will still have times of mourning. These periods of pain continue to teach us about the experience we have been through until we don't need them anymore.

Psychic Numbing

Sometimes when we experience a loss that's great, profound, and quick, we become for a short period of time incapable of feeling. This is called psychic numbing. It can happen when someone dies very suddenly or when several people are wiped out by a tragedy. It is very common among women who find out their husbands are having affairs. Frequently it occurs to the one left when the leaver announces it's time to go.

This anesthetized condition of our feelings is a protection against overwhelming and destructive emotions. Feelings are allowed to surface in a diffused way or only a few at a time. Sometimes a person will admit, "I don't feel anything . . . I feel numb." But slowly and surely this natural psychic anesthetic wears off and the feeling capacity returns. When this happens, we may be very confused or even panicky. In the end, however, a balance will be created. We will be able to handle our emotions and they will return only in manageable amounts.

AWAKENING FEELINGS

Allowing yourself to feel all feelings that arise is the best way to remain in the healing process. Don't pull a defensive sheet over them, hoping they will go to sleep. If you want them out and away, the only window for them to escape through is your awareness. A big feeling can't squeeze out a pinpoint of awareness. Admit the size of the feeling so you can give it the amount of attention it deserves. Only then will you be dealing with it realistically.

Trying to ignore or bury a strong feeling is sure to fail if your goal is maximum emotional recovery.

Some of the feelings ex-spouses most often reported in my survey were:

guilt	anger	embarrassment
shame	loneliness	depression
fear	sadness	hopefulness

It's not only the "down" feelings you want to acknowledge but the "up" emotions, too, which may include:

strength	peacefulness	security
courage	self-compassion	excitement
responsiveness	confidence	hopefulness

Because the down feelings are giving us so much trouble, they tend to crowd the positive emotions off the stage of our attention. But we need to remember that when we experience our healing emotions, they should not be devalued because they don't seem to fit in with our prevailing gloomy mood. To the contrary, positive emotions should be given star billing as reminders that we have much going for us under all our temporary turmoil.

CHARTING DAILY MOODS

All of our feelings are on a continuum. They range from pain to comfort to joy.

Most days our feelings stay in the comfortable range. Deep pain or euphoric happiness are at either end of the spectrum. The process of divorce causes an upset among our "average" feelings and we are bounced every which way. This is normal and to be expected. One day we're up; another we're down. What's important is that we accept ourselves, wherever we are, from day to day.

We can see our own hope in the lives of others. Most of the tremulous feelings experienced by ex-spouses level out within a year after their divorces.

Avoid Medicating Your Feelings

Feelings will heal only as they are expressed. So it is important to avoid medicating and running from these feelings. The temptation is certainly there, most frequently in the form of . . .

You cannot heal what you cannot feel. You cannot feel what you medicate.

alcohol   nicotine
drugs   sugar

Behaviors are often used to achieve the same numbing effect, and we find people getting involved with excessive . . .

eating   spending
working   exercising
busyness   rebounding into relationships

Figure 7.1. Resolution of Post-Divorce Feelings

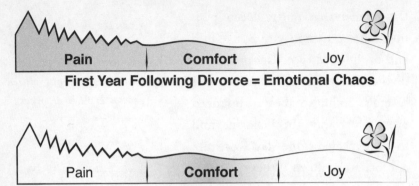

First Year Following Divorce = Emotional Chaos

Returns to Here

Eventual Resolution

SAFE PEOPLE AND PLACES

We all benefit from sharing our feelings, but it helps to be discriminating about the people we go to with our emotions. The best choices are:

Counselors
Support groups
Selected friends
Selected family

Characteristics of safe people include these descriptions:

They do not ridicule.
They do not belittle.
They are not sarcastic.

Be careful not to share everywhere or all the time. Divorce is a process you are going through. It is not the core of your identity or lifestyle. You are more than your identity as a divorced person. As compelling an issue as it is to you now, focusing only on this with family members and friends can be detrimental to your own self-image and your relationships. Don't expect others to feel the degree of your hottest emotions. Don't burden them with your expectations of an emotional response equal to yours. Blame is something we learn to work out best within ourselves or with professional support as we grow in understanding of our marriage experience.

Figure 7.2. Avoid These Ways to Medicate Feelings

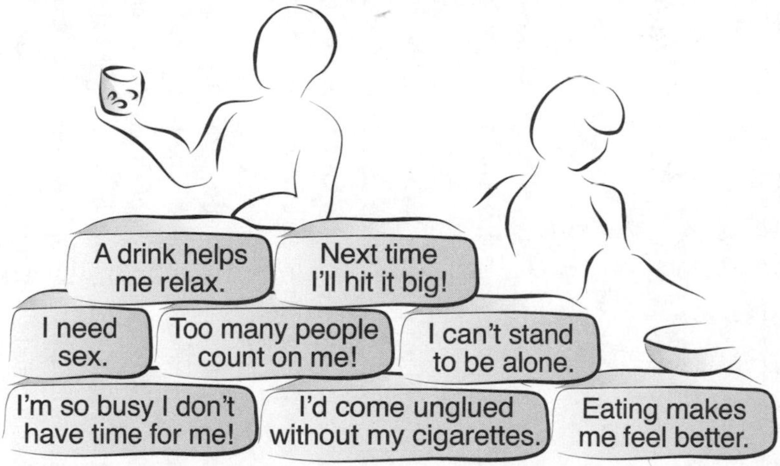

A drink helps me relax.

Next time I'll hit it big!

I need sex.

Too many people count on me!

I can't stand to be alone.

I'm so busy I don't have time for me!

I'd come unglued without my cigarettes.

Eating makes me feel better.

Divorce Ceremony May Aid in Closure

On the following pages, you'll find a sample divorce ceremony, which includes many blame-eliminating statements and acknowledges mutual responsibility for the ending of the relationship, as well as mutual goodwill for the future. It closes with a request for forgiveness and the Serenity Prayer.

OUR *Divorce* CEREMONY

On this day we come together, with some sadness, to accept that our marriage is dissolved.

On _____ (date) in _____ (city and state), we were married. We thought on that day that we were entering a marriage that would be permanent. We had plans, hopes and fears.

What we didn't know and didn't plan on is the fact that we had each come to the marriage with parts of ourelves unknown. These unknowns prevented us from seeing ourselves clearly and also kept us from getting to know one another. As we have grown and changed, we have not been able to grow together. It has become clear that we cannot go on as a couple any longer.

We have tried to give each other love, comfort and support. We did not set out to hurt one another. Guilt, fear, shame and hurt have become a part of our life. There have been many misunderstandings, and at times each of us felt the other was responsible for what was happening. We did not realize that both of us brought pain to the relationship.

Inside each of us were two wounded and frightened children who needed support and healing. Neither of us has been able to give what was needed and perhaps neither of us was able to receive what was needed. We did our best over the years.

After _____ (# of years), we admit defeat. We are not defeated as two individuals; we are simply defeated in making this union work.

We have made a decision to obtain a divorce. Each odf us will find our own way to heal. We will cope and lend support to each other as we go our separate ways.

Even though we could not fulfill our plans as a couple, our prayer is that we will fulfill our separate lives in our own way.

We ask forgiveness of each other, We have each forgiven ourselves and ask that our families, our community and our God support our decision.

THE *Serenity* PRAYER

God grant me the serenity to accept the things I cannot change,
the courage to change the things I can, and the wisdom to know the difference.

—Parts of this ceremony were written by Viginia Lisenbee Davis

One problem in divorce recovery is the lack of closure to the experience. Unlike any other loss of a person, no dignified ceremony marks the end of one experience and the beginning of another. Attending a memorial service after a death, saying good-bye to your classmates at graduation, watching a father "give away" his daughter at her wedding—all of these occasions publicly acknowledge our sadness at an ending as well as hope for a new beginning.

If I had my way, I would have divorce ceremonies preceded by divorce announcements, with people coming together to give support and acknowledgment, helping each person make the transition. There would be no shame or blame. We need to have the option of an open statement of divorce in order to commemorate the fact that there has been a "death" or ending. This important loss deserves a dignified and blameless acknowledgment acted out in ceremony or, at least, documented in some human and social way, not just legally.

We need to incorporate this important milestone into our lives as we each go our separate ways. A formal good-bye to the marriage would emphasize its finality and help boost us out of the past and into the present. By the time we are ready to divorce, everyone knows the negatives and what the pain was like. Focusing on what was good and the importance of letting go of the pain, we could support one another in a much more positive singleness. Probably one of the greatest benefits of a formal divorce would be for the children. They would see their parents being able to part in a dignified ritual, and that the relationship responsible for bringing them into this world was dissolved with respect for its importance to them.

8

LOSSES MAKE LASTING LESSONS

Joan: I carried a big burden of guilt for about ten years after my divorce. It ruled decisions I made for myself and my children. I also spent a lot of time fearing my ex-husband would commit suicide like my father had. Whenever he came to get the children, I would hardly say a word, scared that I would upset him. So whenever there was any accommodating to do, any angry or painful feelings toward him, I would keep them to myself.

In therapy I became conscious that I had taken on this super-responsible attitude toward people, and I learned that this was common among children from substance-abusing families. I wasn't alone and I didn't have to hold on to it. It was an old survival habit from the past. I had the illusion of having some control over chaos. But I found it didn't work, anyway, and I gradually learned to let it go. Divorce brought me to the point where I finally got rid of this problem.

Ken: One of the many lessons I learned was about honesty with my family. I thought this was just something my ex-wife was short on, but I realized it would have helped, also, coming from me with my children. At the time of the divorce, I didn't want them to know why I was leaving their mother. I just couldn't say "I'm leaving you with a woman who plays around because I'm somehow no longer her type." I mean, that's all I could think of then. So naturally, they saw me as the bad guy and she helped reinforce that. She was the wounded lady who was left behind.

The kids still have no knowledge of their mother's affairs and how I may have failed her. I didn't just leave because we had some vague problems. The kids didn't see us argue much. We weren't close enough to argue. If I had used counseling and support from the start, I think I could have been more honest with them about what really happened. Now isn't the right time. Some day . . .

Kathy: It's kind of hard now for me to believe that I thought my life had ended when Jim headed out. I was only twenty-four. It just shows how you can get into a habit of thinking of yourself in only one way. All my teen years, my friends and I thought about how we looked almost every waking hour. It never occurred to us that this wasn't a good attitude to have about ourselves. We thought it showed that we cared about ourselves and about attracting nice guys, not nerds. And it felt so good to be admired. It felt good to be physically active and athletic.

It's obvious to me now that I was really lopsided in what I did and the way I saw myself. Looking good was an easy way to get approval, interest, dates. Whatever else we were or did, I'm sure meant something. I wanted to be known as a nice, friendly person. But I gave very little thought to pursuing whatever else I wanted in life. What could be more important than getting a guy? Now I know.

Bob: The drinking thing would have become worse if the divorce hadn't happened. I can't say the divorce wouldn't have happened if I had stopped drinking, because that was a symptom of the differences between us, not the cause.

Anyway, I wish I had stopped drinking earlier, both for reasons of health and our relationship. Drinking gave me some temporary relief, but it had a permanent effect on my kids' image of me. That's less in their minds, I'm sure, now that alcohol is no longer a part of my life.

Losses of Divorce

Abraham Lincoln may have never gone through divorce, but he once said about losing companions, "I shall at least have one friend left, and that friend shall be down inside me."

In my own life, the losses have at times appeared numerous and overwhelming. The prospect of being alone and a single parent was very frightening. Today in hindsight, I can see that my own experiences with divorce helped shape that new friend I found "down inside me."

Some of the losses we may encounter after divorce are:

Security	Self-Esteem
Companionship	Comfortable routine
Friends	Finances
Family	Hopes and dreams

At the time, these losses seem to stretch to the horizon and preoccupy our days. The most distressing immediate losses I felt were that of family, friends, and security. In 1970, divorce was not as common as it is today. Both friends and family members lacked experience in reacting to someone who was divorced, so they didn't seem to know how to respond. It was as if a death had taken place: many just pulled away. The loneliness and aloneness I experienced at this time pushed me through the door to make new friends. What I learned in the process erased a burden of self-doubt and proved to me that I was capable of making friends and entering new relationships. Many began to accept me just the way I was.

My loss of financial security began to shape my life quite drastically. I needed to take responsibility for myself. I went back to school and started training for a professional future. Little did I know what was in store for me as I ventured out, met new people, and began my profession. Today I'm grateful for the push my insecurities gave me, but back then I didn't have a clue as to the ultimate fulfillment that would result from the losses I was experiencing.

When my familiar routine was no more, I was at first very uncomfortable. Then I began to see that even though my habits were changed a great deal, a host of advantages presented themselves. For instance, I no longer needed to:

- Meet the same schedule
- Fulfill someone else's expectations
- Hide my emotional pain
- Be careful in conversation
- Make excuses

I gained a sense of freedom and opportunity that was new and empowering. I learned to affirm it frequently, which helped me in the healing process.

As I moved from marital status to single status, I experienced quite a shift in self-esteem. At first it seemed like a loss, but as I met each challenge over and over, my appreciation for what I could do grew and grew. The more I did well as a single person, the more confident I became in my own abilities—and the more my self-esteem grew.

REFRAMING LOSSES

Writing down our worries often helps us make them more manageable. Try documenting what you see as your major losses in the past. Then, being very honest with yourself, determine if you gained anything from them. Usually it can't be said that nothing positive came out of a loss, or that nothing was learned that didn't benefit our lives later.

Attitude Choices: Going Up Versus Going Down

We all have the option of going one of two ways with our attitudes after divorce:

Self-Defeating

Blame others: act as a victim and blame your life problems on someone else.

Negative Attitude

Emphasize all the down sides to make things seem worse than they are.

Lack of Focus

Ignore your goals and just live out others' plans for you.

Spend Time with Negative People

Pessimism and criticism are contagious and will weaken your potential and self-esteem.

Expect Failure

You create what you believe, so if you expect to fail, you will.

Self-Esteeming

Take responsibility: let your own values guide you rather than the expectations of others.

Take Credit

Give yourself a pat on the back for your successes and courage.

Set Priorities

Evaluate life by what you have not by what you don't have.

Make New Friends

Look for people you respect and become like them. Follow a positive attitude with positive behavior.

Set Priorities

You create what you believe, so if you expect to succeed, you will.

Don't talk yourself into feeling as if you have no choices about your response to divorce. By changing yourself, you can change your circumstances. That is what empowerment is all about. You can choose to turn your losses into lessons.

Low self-worth people send out messages of pain. They hide their feelings under an appearance of being happy and pleasant.

High self-worth people own all of their feelings and believe it is all right to have all feelings. Their honesty with themselves and others gives them good feelings.

A high self-worth person is:

Sometimes happy

Sometimes angry

Sometimes sad

And whatever the feeling is . . . we are honest with ourselves.

Stretching Your Self-Worth

Self-worth, self-esteem, identity, and self-importance all are terms describing ways of picturing ourselves. They are mental photographs of how we think we are doing on the value scale we have adopted. These images readily show how much we believe in ourselves.

Virginia Satir developed this concept to make an abstract idea more concrete by looking at self-worth in terms of a pot—a three-legged, round, huge, black iron pot. During winter the pot is used to store potatoes. During summer, vegetables and meat are put into the pot for making stew. Another time in the year, it is used for making soap. Two questions always came to mind about the pot and its contents: What is it full of now? How full is it?

This pot image is open to many interpretations. One implication from the image of the pot as self-worth is that a healthy relationship is based on reality. We need to face who we are and how much the other person can realistically give.

Another idea apparent from the illustration is that high-pot people can choose to be generous and positive: they have a lot to give. Low-pot people tend to protect, to guard what little of themselves they have, especially by keeping others far enough away so that no one can see their inadequacies. Their isolation makes them fearful, but it is necessary to keep alive the impression that they are generous.

Another interpretation is that the different ingredients in the pot have varied effects on others. Soap and stew give off good smells and attract people in friendly gatherings. Friendliness is expressed in the sharing of oneself with others after they have shared the products from the pot. People add vegetables and meat. People share the stew in friendship.

Potatoes, on the other hand, when they have been stored too long, can rot and emit a rather offensive odor. People want them out of their lives. The pot of neglected potatoes is similar to behavior that keeps people away. The level of one's self-worth gives out messages. It is similar to the quantity and quality of materials in our pot.

Choices to Change, Broaden Security

Grabbing the opportunity to make choices is an exciting part of our divorce recovery. We will make some mistakes, but if we keep trying and risking, many new possibilities will come into our lives.

As we trust ourselves, we find our security becoming more firm.

We cannot expect to move forward all at once. We will, in time, develop the confidence that we will recover wholeness.

Security, which is a basic need for each of us, will broaden. Even with a divorce, our security cannot be taken away because it is based on belief in ourselves and only we own that belief. Security is grounded not only in our capacity to cope and survive but in our ability to make choices.

9
DIVORCE AND FRIENDSHIP

here are three kinds of friends: The intimate and faithful friend who would walk over coals and rearrange his or her life to be there for you (or even give you a place to stay during the transition); the friend who would offer you advice, suggest a few good books to read, invite you out to dinner, or bring you a bottle of wine and listen to what you have to say; and the friend who will suggest a counselor, send you cards, and call you weekly. My experience is that most friends fall into the third category.

When the divorcing couple makes their announcement to split, friends are backed into an extremely awkward position. Who can really blame them for taking sides? Is it even possible to remain friends with both partners? Usually, it is not.

Traditionally, one partner usually starts the friendship, and that partner is typically closer to the friend than the spouse is. What tends to happen is that each friend reverts back to the original relationship that he or she had when the pair were first introduced as a couple. It's a natural process most of the time. When difficulties arise in the divorcing couple's life, they often go to the friend they were originally close to and when the divorce finally happens, it's not a big surprise to the original friend.

> Some information simply does not translate.
> You had to have been there.
> EDWARD MITCHELL

Many factors put distance between the divorcing couple and friends. Not all will necessarily play a role in your relationships, yet the reasons why distance can develop are understandable. If you have children, many of your friendships have been established with other couples who have children. You share babysitters, drive in carpools, go to ballgames, or take dance lessons together. You share experiences. Your friendships develop with those who have similar interests. You tend to be about the same age and at the same time in your life. However, when a divorce takes place, friends are pressured into making a decision to stay friends with one of you, both of you, or maybe neither one of you. The latter being an easy way to avoid having to pick between the two.

One often asks, "Why can't they remain friends with both people?" Gender usually plays a factor. When everyone is married, all the rules are set. When a divorce takes place, it is a little difficult for two friends of the opposite sex to take their kids to a ballgame when one of them is still married. What might people say, and, frankly, what feelings might be evoked? Who wants to get tangled up in the possibilities? This is no one's fault. It is just the way it is.

Consider Sue and Matt. For years, the couples had taken their boys to basketball practice together. Most of the time, it was both couples. Occasionally, one couldn't make it and a threesome carried on. Then Sue and her husband divorced.

The threesome worked for a while; however, if Matt's wife, Jane, had to work late, Sue and Matt would often take the boys. At first their conversations revolved solely around basketball, but over time, they were more personal. Soon Jane became threatened, and when she shared with Matt her feeling uncomfortable and left out, he confided that he, too, felt out of place and was beginning to develop strange feelings toward Sue. Matt became protective of her, concerned about her well-being, and finally he admitted that there was more to his and Sue's relationship than just basketball.

Fortunately for Jane and Matt, they saw the potential danger and decided to rethink their relationship with Sue. While it was very painful for all three of them, Jane and Matt knew that this arrangement was not going to work if they were going to protect their marriage. In this case, it was beneficial that all three people understood, and Jane and Sue were able to keep their friendship in a different form. They had lunches together and occasionally ran or walked together, avoiding future problems. Sadly, not every situation turns out this well.

> Snowflakes are a fragile thing individually,
> but look at what they can do when they stick together.
> FERNANDO BONADVENTURE

Sometimes in a divorce, we find what I call "the shunning" aspect. It comes in many forms and is a technique used as a way of eliminating the divorced person from social events. One reason a person may be shunned is if the divorcing spouse is attractive. This person becomes a threat to every couple in the circle, often perceived as lonely and available. Every attractive divorced person can tell horror stories as men and women (married or not) assume she or he is available and eager for a drink, a weekend away, or something similar. It is degrading, hurtful, and all too frequent. The shunning of this person from group get-togethers comes because wives and husbands are afraid that divorce is catchy. If she or he were invited, perhaps it would put thoughts into the minds of the other couples, potentially threatening those relationships, too.

A feeling of having a fifth wheel or a sense of being off balance at couple-oriented dinners and parties can occur, leading to downright snubs from familiar friends. However, there are a few benefits. Cindy told me in a therapy session that it's important to find the upside whenever you can. She finds it gratifying to be able to tell stories at dinner parties and talk as much as she wants to without someone there to correct her. Charles says it is nice to stop and have a drink with friends after work without feeling guilty. It is common for people to discover that their level of social interaction changes. It doesn't have to be bad or hard; it is just different.

Friends' Viewpoints

Divorce can end the best of friendships, and it is important for those being divorced to approach the subject directly with mutual friends. Talking to mutual friends and letting them know how you feel and that you value their friendship makes the difference between support and loss. Let them know you want to remain friends with each of them, even though they are no longer part of a couple. It is important for you to share that you do not intend to choose between them. They can both continue their friendship with you if they so choose.

Let them know you would like to spend time with them—dinner, drinks, a movie, or other activities you used to do as a couple. Keep what feels good, familiar, and nonthreatening. This is a time to talk about gender issues. Though difficult to talk about directly, it is a good time to state that you hope to see each of them individually to continue your friendship. However, because of emotional difficulties and other people's observations, it might be more appropriate for you to be seen moving forward in gender appropriate friendships—two women or two men. Oftentimes, it is just the better way to go. This is an individual situation, of course, and must be handled with discretion.

You can share with the divorcing couple that you want to be there for them, but the details of the divorce are theirs alone. You do not want to hear all the details or make any judgments about what

happened. Treat the divorce with respectful privacy. Let your divorcing friends know you care. Send cards, offer to help them move, or
invite them to couple parties. (Note: When you are inviting both of
them to a party, let them know if his or her ex-partner is expected to
be there. That way, he or she can choose whether or not to attend.)

Do take a stand and let each one know that you intend to remain
friends with both of them, if that is indeed your intention. Change
the subject if one partner starts to bash the other. It is dangerous
for all concerned to enter into these kinds of discussions. Tell both
friends ahead of time that you will not engage in any conversation
that reflects badly on either of them.

Divorcing Couple's Point of View

This will be a time of assessing and coming to terms with the
people you want to keep in your life, who you want to be close to,
and with whom you want to limit or end relationships entirely. Each
relationship is unique; therefore, how you handle each one will be
as well. You, and only you, will know where you want to draw your
support, trust, and understanding.

> The divorce process may cause us to lose friends,
> but we find new friends. Some friends become
> like family and become very close friends.
> True friends become closer and bonding takes place.
>
> CATHY MICHALSON

The following guidelines may help you to continue or reestablish
those friendships you decide to keep:

- Tell your friends that their friendships are very important
  to you and you hope to find a way to make it work. Let

them know that you are aware it will be different, but you
just aren't sure how different it will be. Explain to them that
you are divorcing your partner not your friends.

- Spend time individually with each of your friends, as time
  allows. Lunches are a great time to connect. Try to incorporate
  activities like walking and hiking. Not only do you get the
  extra health benefits of exercising, but these activities also tend
  to be less emotionally draining than just sitting and talking.
- Ask for help. If you are relocating or making a large purchase,
  you can ask friends for help in the decision-making process.
  Let them know that you value their opinion.
- If your children are not going to have a day-to-day mom or
  dad, one of the kindest offers you can make is to do some
  activities with the children. Role models are going to
  become very important.

Over time, some friendships will grow and others will fade. Some
might end altogether, as was the case with Carla's relationships. She
had been part of a six-couple personal-growth group. The twelve of
them had spent two years sharing their lives, discussing their hopes,
dreams, conflicts, and joys. When the group aspect ended, the six
couples remained very close friends. They spent holidays together,
went on camping trips, and occasionally took vacations together.
Their children all grew up together.

Several years into the friendship, Jim decided he wanted to leave his
marriage. Jim told the family he was going to leave them and eventually marry the accountant for the firm. He made both announcements
just before Christmas. It devastated Carla and brought great pain to
all four children. When Jim left, it was a painful time for everyone.

The group, which had spent the last several holidays together
(in part because many lived great distances from their biological

families), was due to plan Christmas Day together. When Carla asked where the planning session was going to take place, she sensed hesitation from her closest friend. Finally, the friend explained that Carla and her family were not invited to be part of the holiday season. She went on to say that while Carla was now single, attractive, and lonely, she might feel uncomfortable around the men who would be there. The women had discussed it over lunch and concluded that Carla should not attend.

Carla was shocked at first, then hurt, and finally she accepted this decision from a group of women who had been her intimate friends for years. With help from a competent therapist, Carla came to understand that it was not she who was rejected. While it was a painful lesson, it may just have been that these women were threatened to have an attractive, intelligent, and caring person in their midst. Ultimately, those relationships ended completely.

> It is up to you to surround yourself
> with people who will support your journey.
>
> CLAUDIA BLACK

Bill had a different experience. He and his wife had actively participated in their community. He coached basketball, and he and his wife golfed once a week with other couples in the community. When Sara decided she was going to leave the marriage, Bill was crushed. They had been together a long time, and most of their friends were couples living in their neighborhood.

Sara asked Bill to leave not only his marriage but the family home as well. She felt that it was important for the children to stay in familiar surroundings. Bill felt adrift. He left and rented an apartment while he thought things through. He continued to meet with his basketball group and play golf with the male partners of the couples he and his wife were friends with. Finally, he hit on a decision for himself. He went back to his neighborhood and rented the smallest house available. Not only could his children go back and forth between both parents' homes, but he could keep his friends as well.

It has been a few years now, and Sara and Bill have found it to be the perfect solution. Sara was not invested in Bill's leaving his children nor leaving his friends. The relationships have all changed somewhat, but thankfully the divorcing couple found a way to make their lives work and their friends were not forced to make a choice between the two of them.

> Everything you live through
> makes you the person you are now.
>
> UNKNOWN

How Friends Can Help

Be a good listener. Set boundaries. You don't really want to hear the intimate details of the divorce. You simply want to be there for your friend. It's not important to provide answers. In fact, offering advice is sometimes detrimental. Simply listen and offer support to whatever your friend is sharing. Offer hope with examples of how much faith you have in your friend's ability to come through this tough time.

If you don't like the story of your life, change it. You are the star of your story.

Provide as much help to the divorced couple's children as possible. This is a highly traumatic time for them, and having someone who is strong and interested in their lives is an exceptional gift. Both parents will appreciate anything that can be done to lessen the pain for the children.

Talking to your divorcing friends about their option for mediation, which is sometimes a better choice than hiring an attorney, could be helpful.

Keep reminding your friend that this event is not the end of the world. It just feels like it. Tell stories of others you have known who survived a divorce. We all know people. You might even share some stories of people who not only survived but also thrived after a divorce and found parts of themselves that blossomed in their new lives.

Friends can be the greatest support to someone who is divorcing.

10

MOST EX-SPOUSES AGREE: DIVORCE IS A POSITIVE FORCE

Joan: Sometimes I think it's good we can't see ahead. We'd be overwhelmed. Still, I wish I had known at the time of my divorce how many doors it was going to open for me. I never would have believed it. I went back to school, got two degrees, and became a professional. I never planned on that happening. I never thought I had the ability to do that. As a result of that and all the other things that happened to me, I feel it made me a much more whole person. I reach out to people much more now. I don't feel nervous if I'm not in control of everything.

After I started believing in myself, I came to a much greater realization of the ultimate goodness of the whole universe. When I opened myself to opportunities, they came. It made me believe in a master plan for all of us. I started allowing myself the luxury of finding out what my plan was all about. In a way, my divorce led to a new sense of spirituality.

Ken: My divorce really opened my eyes. It was a case of better late than never. I had been really stuck in a role with a lifestyle everyone approved of, but some part of reality was missing. I had always thought that an important part of being successful was having a beautiful woman at my side. Okay, so the woman is gone, but not only that, everything I worked for went with her. Of course, that was my own decision, but there I was with nothing that I thought mattered anymore. So I had to either convince myself that I still mattered or just wallow in my losses. It was a clear-cut choice and the wallowing was hurting my work.

I had to get over the idea that I was coming home to an empty apartment. It wasn't empty. I was there! Counseling helped me reinforce that. Being by myself really became okay. Being myself—looking and feeling my best, doing what I want to—well, to me that is gratifying now.

Kathy: Divorce was a stretch. It forced me into taking action. I never felt I had special abilities for a career. But I went back to school because I knew I had to make a living and college graduates get better pay. I took a computer course because everything's about computers now. I was surprised! I liked computers. I went into computer programming, and I also found I had other skills. Management was one. I really turned on to the whole process of getting ahead, getting a good job. And I did.

For the first time in my life, I felt as if I could be independent. I wasn't waiting to go out with some popular guy now as my big thing. I was doing less dating than in high school. And now I'm getting less exercise, although that's still real important for me. But I'm far more conscious now of the fact that I'm more than how I look.

Bob: I still have a letter from my attorney stating that he had to put in writing his opposition to my decision to give up everything and that it ran against his advice. He said he felt it was a very poor move. That's an understatement. If I had it to do over again—heaven forbid—I would go to counseling first to get a stronger sense of self-worth. I needed approval too much from everyone. And I didn't think my needs were at all important. Then there was the guilt thing. If I hadn't made her pull up roots, maybe my wife wouldn't have started running around. But maybe she would have anyway.

The AA community did a great deal for me. I met people there who valued me. If I had concentrated earlier on other friends who weren't such drinkers, I would have avoided some problems. The negativity of my old friends in the past had dragged me down. But I had been too busy and lazy back then to make new friends.

The reality has set in. A future full of question marks looms ahead. Now's the time when we'd really like to hear from others who have walked this way before us. What do both the leavers and the left have to say about this crisis of divorce after they have reached the ranks of survivors?

In my work as a therapist, I have surveyed 200 people about their divorces and what influences divorce had in their lives. Over the years I have worked with many couples who have been through various stages of relationship following divorce. Some have divorced; some have remarried; some are adult children from divorced families. Among their responses I have looked for patterns that might help others in healing from painful relationships and the divorce process. There is a general agreement about the best advice to give the recently separated, and about the benefits that divorce ultimately produces. While they admitted it wasn't all easy and upbeat, the majority of those who responded felt divorce was a positive occurrence in their lives.

As we all agree, there's no doubt divorce is one of the most painful and emotionally draining events in a lifetime. But as the shock, the hurt, and the numbness begin to subside, the ability to function does return. Function then leads to adjustment. This adjustment is the direct result of taking action. This action springs from allowing movement and transition to happen, rather than clinging to dreams and worn-out patterns.

Ex-Spouses' Reactions and Advice

Divorce recovery takes time. We grow a little each day, despite not being able to make the great leaps and bounds we'd like to. Here are eight ways ex-spouses in the survey reacted to the main issues of divorce:

1. *Get clear about your contribution to the marriage and the divorce.* Recognize that when a divorce takes place,

both parties have contributed to the deterioration of the relationship. As we look at our own part of the problem, blame gets reduced. When there is less blame, it becomes easier to negotiate, adjust, and move on.

A second reason to explore one's role is that everything learned about our own part in the coming together, the life shared, and the reasons for the divorce will come in handy if we enter into another relationship.

2. *Avoid entering another relationship for a year.* You will ride so many emotional merry-go-rounds as a part of the divorce that it's good to give intense feelings a rest before going into another relationship. Right after having surgery, would you go on a hiking vacation? Let your emotional healing happen before taking on intense and important feelings in a new close friendship.

3. *Develop a support system.* A divorce often changes social networks. Some couples' friends feel as though they have to take sides. Some relatives of one's ex-partner may change their attitudes. It's important to start your own support system free of entanglements.

During this time, if at all possible, join a support group in your area. Many different kinds of groups are available.

The best move you can make is to contact a therapist, who can help you find either a therapy group or a support group in addition to serving as your sounding board. You can take all your hurt, anger, and any other feelings you might be experiencing to therapy. A therapist's training can help you put it all together to obtain a new perspective.

Making new friends should be on your agenda, too. Reach out and share life with new people.

4. *Face reality.* Not facing reality is why most marriages end. The time comes to look at matters the way they are and not the way we wish they were. So often we hang on to a

remote hope, a thread, or a myth. At some point it becomes necessary to sever that last fragile link and transfer energy from hanging on to letting go.

5. *Be willing to face difficult times with children.* Children are in a tough spot in all divorces. They face various concerns, such as money, loyalty, or feelings. Keeping your issues, feelings, and needs quite separate from those of your children will help. It is critical to let them know their needs are important, but don't lose sight of the fact that this is your divorce. If you meet your own needs, you will be a stronger, more able person to meet theirs. If you don't, no one will be happy.

Children need to know that takes time to work out everyone's needs. Meanwhile you can be the role model they'll need later in life by equipping yourself in all ways to function best as head of the family.

6. *Take the opportunity to grow in self-worth.* Self-worth comes, in part, from knowing you can care for yourself. Regardless of your past sense of self-worth, divorce offers the opportunity to develop a healthy opinion of who you are. During divorce recovery we are catapulted into an opportunity that demands we develop every resource we have. As we succeed, we feel better and better about ourselves. These good feelings will foster and increase self-worth.

Some people in my survey made these comments on self-worth:

Eilene, 36: "Reestablishing myself has begun a new adventure in life."

John, 54: "I faced myself, hit bottom, and started up. I panicked, I fell, and picked myself up. Today I fly strong and bold, surrounded by people who like me. And I like myself."

Jill, 48: "I feel good about myself and my achievements."

Bonnie, 39: "My self-esteem has greatly improved since achieving success independently."

Cynthia, 48: "I learned to become a whole person. I learned to take risks. Today I like who I am and learn to love myself more each day."

Nicole, 47: "I am able to see my growth both personally and professionally. I have many new supportive friends."

Mitchell, 43: "My self-worth is fantastic now."

Toby, 36: "Today I have found myself. Prior to the divorce I was only someone's daughter, wife, mother."

Ray, 37: "Because of the activities I was forced to undertake, and did so successfully, I have become a much stronger, confident person."

7. **Develop fulfilling relationships.** The majority of people responding to the survey highlighted the importance of developing honest, direct, and nurturing relationships. It's important to invest time and energy in as many family relationships as possible. Siblings, aunts, uncles, and grandparents also become involved in the family changes. Whenever you can, keep and nurture relationships. The more support you have, the faster you will heal. On the other hand, if the relationships are blaming and add more pain and stress to your life, you may need to let them go.

When developing new relationships, you may want to look for mentors as well as support: people you'd like to have share their secrets of success with you. These may be people you can talk to or people you see or hear about whose achievements in the face of obstacles can be recalled for inspiration.

The people in my survey said this on the value of relationships in divorce recovery:

Ted, 43: "I have found friends who accept me."

Fay, 29: "I have more honest relationships with my children."

Yvonne, 51: "I have learned to know the value of three or four good friends rather than lots of acquaintances."

Andrea, 36: "I have made new friends who support me in my struggles, have fun with me, and help me celebrate my victories."

8. **Face and express your feelings.** Many feelings need to be felt and expressed during this very tumultuous time. Feelings that do not get expressed become painful attitudes that are self-defeating.

- Anger not expressed becomes depression.
- Hurt not expressed becomes permanent sadness.
- Fears not expressed become avoidance.
- Inadequacies not expressed become phony smiles.

All feelings have purpose. Feel them, and express them in a safe, nurturing place. This is where the value of support groups and a therapist becomes important. Expressing deep and painful feelings must be done, and yet it's not appropriate to share many of these feelings with children, relatives, and friends. Even closest friends do not want to know the depth of some feelings.

Through my survey of ex-spouses, I heard about much healing as time passed:

Libby, 49: "I was so angry in the early days. I'm grateful I was able to express that anger to my therapist and turn my energy toward my own growth."

Angela, 40: "I thought I was going to cry forever. Then one day, I dried my tears and went on. Some days a special song or holiday will bring tears again, but most of the time I feel great."

Cristy, 38: "My fears of loneliness have really been relieved in the last few months. In the beginning I think I felt lonely because of all the change. I don't feel that way anymore."

Tom, 50: "My early hurt healed as I looked more closely at what happened. I could more easily see both of our contributions. My hurt turned to sadness, and today that sadness has healed."

My Own (and Others') Best Recovery Tools

1. *Good friends.* Making the time to see friends was crucial for me. I lost some and gained some, but the friends who stuck with me were the most honest and sincere.
2. *Prayer.* There were some times when only faith in God could comfort me, and it was what I sought. While I hated much of the divorce process, I found peace and comfort in developing a spiritual life for myself. Now that I've achieved some distance, I can see much sense and order in all that happened. I am grateful for my growth and the belief I have in spirituality. Whatever name you give to a Higher Power, drawing on this spiritual source can be an antidote for the initial loneliness and powerlessness we experience.
3. *Ask for help.* I used to think I could do everything by myself. Today I know that this personal myth is part of my belief that no one was trustworthy, that no one would be there for me. During the divorce crisis I learned to ask, receive, and accept help. Most of the people I have talked to expressed just how wonderful being able to reach out was for them.
4. *Relief from indecision and tension.* Many of the ex-spouses in my survey reported that they experienced months (sometimes years) of anxiety and stress coming from indecision. I, too, was afraid of making mistakes and vacillated over what action to take until I was a wreck. Finally, I learned that very few mistakes are irreversible and that when I did act, action brought relief and more energy. In time, I also learned to trust myself—only because I acted and

saw the results, which were usually just fine. It took action to prove I could trust in myself.

5. *Books, tapes, workshops.* The bookstores are full of guides and help for people who want to grow and change. Many people in my survey reported they got a great deal of support and direction from the printed word. Over half of my respondents mentioned that weekend and weeklong workshops were helpful in building skills.

6. *Develop new hobbies and recreations.* Again, almost everyone I heard from started new activities for themselves. These activities helped to relieve stress, divert attention from problems, and they offered opportunities to meet new friends, not to mention providing pleasure. Activities people mentioned as positive included:

- Dancing
- Music lessons
- Fly-fishing
- Traveling
- Volunteer work
- Horseback riding

7. *Explore your family-of-origin issues.* This certainly is high on my list of ways to make progress personal. More than half of the people I surveyed said that divorce raised questions about the past, which prompted exploration. As this questioning took place, my surveyed ex-spouses reported that they were learning about themselves in a way that had not been available to them earlier.

Divorce brings many old family patterns to the surface. When we look at, and learn to understand, childhood emotional baggage that we are still carrying, we see the origins of several misunderstandings. Many marriage and family therapists have said that innumerable divorces could have been prevented if the partners had previously divorced their families of origin. This is not to say that families were to blame; it only indicates that much is to be learned from detaching from family patterns.

8. *Take care of your body.* Sometimes after divorce we are very vulnerable to practices that are bad for our bodies, and I was no exception. When feelings are troubled, it is easy to overeat or undereat. Sometimes depression stalls our exercise efforts. Respondents to my survey reported that they felt most healthy and strong when they ate well, slept enough, and exercised regularly.

Some got new haircuts. Many reported that getting rid of old clothes and choosing a new look helped a great deal. Since many people miss the physical touch and presence of the person who was in their lives, three-quarters of the surveyed ex-spouses said a massage enjoyed periodically helped fill that void. Today most health clubs offer professional massage to their members, making it a convenient way of pampering ourselves.

Ways We Have Grown

Divorcing ex-partners commented in the survey on how much better they thought their lives had become after divorcing. Fay said, "Since my divorce, and all the emotions it's brought out among us, I have been able to be more open with each of my children. We talk about real and practical things. They come to me more easily and share themselves with me. The tension in our home is relieved and communication has become more open."

With Marianne, financial independence became a pleasure: "To be totally responsible for myself, to be able to do it, gives me a great deal of self-worth. It feels so free to be in charge of my time, my work, and my money. I feel like an independent, whole person."

Wynne appreciated learning how to take care of both physical and emotional needs without a live-in partner: "No longer do I depend on someone to make me happy. I've learned how to get my needs met, how to make friends, and how to care for myself. I've grown to respect and appreciate myself."

What Parents Learned to
Tell Their Children About Divorce

Children are often a mysterious and troubling complication to the newly divorced. What to tell them? What to do about them? I asked survey participants to share advice they wished their children had received at the time of the divorce. They would have counseled them sooner to:

"Stay out of the middle!"

"The divorce is between your parents. You will never know all that went on with your parent," one father said he would have told his boys.

One mom did tell her daughter, "Each of us will need a separate relationship with you. Do your best to give us that chance to have different ways, different rules."

"Do not carry messages!"

"Be clear with each parent that you want to be yourself with them, not the voice of someone else, and if that is going to be possible, then you cannot carry messages between them." Message carrying leads to various forms of trouble, many ex-spouses agreed.

"Find a good, safe friend to share with!"

Parents wished their children had more people to turn to than just them, such as a peer, a teacher, a relative, or an adult friend recommended by the parent. "Find someone you can trust and share your feelings with that person," one ex-spouse advised her fourteen-year-old daughter. "You need someone besides your parents to share with. This is important for you."

"Accept that you have been through a big trauma, and find as much help as you need to adjust to it and become stronger."

Parents in the survey thought that children, if at all possible, should have professional care, such as a therapist, a support group, or a school counselor. Jean, a mother of three, told her children, "It's okay to get some ideas from a counselor when your life is changing, when it's feeling strange and you are confused."

"Tell yourself each day that the divorce is between your parents and is not your fault."

If your children remember only one thing about their parents' parting, this should be it. Because child-rearing problems are so often mentioned in pre-divorce arguments, children need to know that their parents' problems were not about them but about each other.

Children who are encouraged to take advantage of various sources of help are likely to reach out sooner as adults and not carry crippling emotional burdens in order to prove their self-worth. They will learn that no matter how much input they get from others, they themselves must remain in charge of learning and acting on the advice that feels right for them.

11

HELPING CHILDREN
COPE WITH DIVORCE

Joan: I think the effects of divorce on children can be both positive and negative. If you gave away your right to child support as I did, you have to work hard to give them things, and work even harder to make time for them. My remarriage solved the companionship problem, but since my second husband wasn't earning a lot, I still needed to put in many hours at work.

I took my three kids into my second marriage. I was very fortunate that my second husband really loved them, even though he wasn't in a position to help support them. But he was there for them emotionally and physically. My job took me away from home a lot so this was good in one sense. In another sense, I lost out on some of the important years with my children. But they did have a good male influence, and even after my second marriage ended in divorce, he remained good friends with my children for some of the critical years.

Ken: After divorcing, I messed up with the kids during their teens. I had a daughter and three boys. I really overprotected them, bought them everything. I got my daughter involved in my business. She wanted to make some money, and we got along well. She met all my business associates and was an asset to me. She became very protective of me, controlling my hours, my eating, and making sure I took care of myself. That felt good, to be taken care of again, but as time passed, it became too much. It even got in the way of my relationship with my boys. If they needed something from me, she'd tell them I was busy and not let me know. Things like that began to happen.

So I went back to counseling. It was almost like going through another divorce, but I had to get some breathing space for my life. My daughter wound up in counseling, too. Awful as it all was, I'd say we both learned a lot about ourselves that will come in handy in the future.

Kathy: Four years after my divorce I married Karl. He had two young children, ages five and seven. I hadn't really been on my own very long when I found myself with three new people in my life. In the summer we were all together. During the school year we shared custody with the children's mother. This caused all kinds of difficulties, but we had plenty of good times, too.

I knew there would be many things to learn about being a mom with children past the toddler stages. The main thing I figured out is that the first people to consider are my husband and myself when troubles come up. If we can keep our relationship clear and are open and honest with each other, it seems like together we can handle almost any problems with the kids. When we aren't this way, then almost any problem can divide us. Becoming more of my own person gave me a better idea of how families should work. I know my priorities now.

Bob: I had lots of problems with the kids, but most of them resulted from the bitterness of the divorce. My ex was vocal and aggressive in letting the children know how she felt about their father. This, of course, put the kids in an awkward position. I had to defend myself, which meant putting her down. Otherwise, I felt I'd be seen as a total wimp.

My daughter says she has the hardest time in her own arguments with people because she doesn't know what to say or do except walk away. She's in counseling and that's helping. I think my kids are going to work out what they need to do. I've come to terms with not being able to role model every single issue positively for them. I'm human and they'll be human as parents, too. But I'm glad that I've set an example for my boys about getting help when things get out of hand.

It is easier to build strong children
than to repair adults later in life.

ANN DOUGLAS

Every day thousands of young children become hurt, perplexed, confused, angry, and afraid when they find out their parents are getting divorced. How they respond to this news will depend on how their parents inform them and follow through with the entire process. It will also depend on their ages, the support systems they have, and their personalities.

Every divorce is different and all circumstances are different, but much is similar, as well. For some children, divorce will be a wound that never quite heals and impacts their future lives in ongoing ways: difficulty with their own intimate relationships, development of fears, lack of trust, control issues, and more.

For other children, the divorce brings a reduction to the stress in their lives, they find new ways to cope, they mature early, they become determined in the way they live their lives, and they gain clarity on what they want for their futures. They take this life-altering event and make the most of it. They might experience two happier homes, two happier parents, and many more experiences and possibilities than they might have had in one painful home. They learn to cope with stress and loss and become more flexible and tolerant adults.

We evolve at the rate of the tribe we are plugged into.

CAROLINE MYSS

Telling the Children About the Divorce

When the first steps toward divorce are taken, we need to be able to tell our children that things are not going well between us and our spouses, tough as it may be. This will give the children a chance to grieve appropriately for their changing family. Although it is not a pleasant prospect, it is one that we should not try to prevent. Prolonging the news until the last minute and then suddenly confronting a child with the physical realities of the split is more of a shock. Explain to the child what is happening and in words that children can understand; all the details don't have to be spelled out. Be honest about your feelings. Tell them that you're sad, that you're hurt. Tell them that you, as parents, are not agreeing about many things and you no longer love each other in the same way you did before.

COMMUNICATE RIGHT FROM THE START

Talk to your children as soon as the decision is made to live apart. If possible this is best done with both parents present. Practice by telling a trusted friend or a therapist so that you are not caught up in anger, blame, or guilt while you are actually talking to your children. Assure the children that their lives will remain as much the same as possible. It's only the parents' lives that are going to change.

Children need to be told that none of the changes nor the divorce has anything to do with them. This is a situation between only the parents. Nothing is their fault. This message might have to be given over and over. The children might blame their own bickering, not doing their chores, that they cost money, and use up the parents time. They might see themselves as too much of a responsibility to the parents. Parents will need to keep reassuring the children that none of this is their fault.

About 65 to 70 percent of all the children I have worked with felt that, one way or another, they were part of their parents' divorce. Children need to know that they didn't cause this problem and they cannot fix it either. Make it very, very clear to them that the divorce is between the adults and not between parents and children. This understanding is crucial to the children's self-worth.

Tell them that adults can change the way that they love each other and sometimes cannot agree on very important things. It then becomes necessary to live apart and go through a divorce. What is important to emphasize at this time is that the bond between parents and children is different from that of a married couple. When parents and children do not agree, they do not divorce. It is important that they understand that parents and children are bonded for life. That is part of the parent-child bond. Later in life, they may continue to disagree but will hopefully continue to love each other. Although most don't admit it, many children are often concerned about their parents divorcing them.

Questions That Children Will Wonder About

- Who will I live with?
- How and when will I see my other parent?
- Will I go to the same school?
- Can I see my friends?
- Do parents hate or like each other?
- Is everything the same for my brother(s) and sister(s)?
- How will we do vacations?
- Do we have enough money?
- Did I do something wrong?
- Why did this happen?
- What does Grandma and Grandpa think?

Give the children enough information to know how the changes are going to affect their daily lives. Give some information as you tell them about the separation or divorce. By talking openly and directly to them, it opens the door for them to ask questions. Try to answer them with as much information as their age and temperament allow. The more that is in the open, the more that trust will be protected; however, keep it simple enough for them to understand. Younger children need less information than older children do.

Let them know you have some of those answers but maybe not all of them yet. Be as honest as you can and invite them to come to you (both parents) and ask as many questions as they want. All answers need to be age and privacy appropriate. In the case of a cheating spouse, you might need some professional advice on when and how to handle the situation. No one will be served by saying things that will cause lifelong pain for a child. Each situation needs to be evaluated and acted upon with everyone's best interest in mind.

Recovery for Children of Divorce

When children are made aware that divorce is becoming a reality, their number one need is to feel secure and blameless. Their world—seemingly beyond their control—is toppling, and more than you suspect, they are probably aware of the history of arguments and growing loss of affection.

ADDRESS THEIR NEEDS

They desperately need you to help reduce the trauma with reassurances that:

- It is not their fault.
- The divorce is between both parents, not parents and children.

- They will be safe in terms of home, money, and school; no more surprises.
- You will love them no matter what.
- You want to hear their feelings.
- You will tell them what's going on that concerns them.
- You can't fix everything.

These are the basics of safety during divorce recovery for children. Whether children are young, adolescent, or adult, they are part of a divorce process. Their emotional involvements need to be addressed and shouldn't be minimized, despite the difficulties involved. Very often the children aren't informed that the parents' divorce is in the offing. Including them early in the separation lets them get used to the idea gradually, reducing shock. They need ample assurance that your love for them is secure and can't go away. Children are especially emotional about divorce, but studies show they are also resilient after it occurs.

For many people, a divorce means that their relationship with their partner has been totally and completely ended. That is how it needs to be in many cases for practical and emotional reasons; however, there are many people for whom divorce means some continued contact, particularly if the couple shares children of any age. As divorced parents, we can benefit tremendously by getting a head start on what can be expected in parenting after divorce, both in our roles as single parents and when our ex-spouses become involved.

AFFIRM YOUR LOVE FOR THEM

Find ways to affirm your children on a daily basis. Maybe you need to say to them, "I love you just the way you are," and, "I cherish the fact that you are with me as we all go through this together."

Support one another. Saying, "You are the most important thing in my life right now" will win a response you need. Continue to let them know they are cherished and loved, and that your feelings for them are not going to change.

Children may worry that you could stop loving them, too. They should hear that there was a time when the parents loved each other a whole lot and that they were born out of that love . . . but things change for adults. Even though Mom and Dad do not love each other in the way that they need to as a husband and a wife, nothing can change the love of their own children.

The Children's Response

Once you have had this initial interaction, the children may respond in many different ways. Most of the time they may exhibit some denial, sometimes outward anger, sometimes inner depression, silence, lots of tears, trouble sleeping, or acting out behavior. These are the times to reassure them that you understand that they have many feelings and you will listen to all of those feelings.

Encourage them to keep asking questions, and let them know that they can also talk to a trusted and beloved grandparent, aunt, uncle, etc. You will understand that they want to talk to someone other than either of you.

If negative behavior becomes part of their reaction, it has to be faced and handled. For a while, you might give them the benefit of the doubt and overlook some mild payback; however, serious negative behavior must be handled in the same way you had previously handled it.

Hurt and pain are not excuses for negative or punishing behavior. Sometimes the reaction is delayed. It may come out in indirect ways: school problems, problems with friends, or, very often, some kind of self-punishment (not eating, accident prone, excess eating, not sleeping, bed-wetting, etc.). These are serious issues that require supportive help from a counselor or therapist.

Tips and Tools for Parents

- Do not argue or blame in front of the children.
- Try to keep the child's daily routines with as little disruption as possible.
- Get professional help to work out strong differences in opinion, and keep children totally unaware of how much disagreement you each experience. Have these difficult discussions outside of the home.
- Keep home as peaceful and as consistent as possible so the child/children can feel a space of safety and comfort.
- Keep all grandparents in the child's life, if possible. Be clear with the grandparents that if they are an important part of the child's life, they must support both parents and not take sides. This is very important. Grandparents can be the consistency that the child needs but only if they support both parents. If not, then grandparent visits need to be monitored by the opposite parent.
- Do your best to divide time between both parents.
- Be honest and talk with children about some of the necessary changes. What they fear might be much bigger than what they actually know.
- Eat together, do chores together, and handle your own emotions and loss with someone outside the family.

EXPECT DENIAL AND ALLOW HEALING

Parents can expect that their children may deny the fact of divorce for a while. Denial is a natural protective process that often occurs whenever a death takes place. Divorce, in many ways, is like a death in the family. Let them deny the situation, but keep letting them know your feelings and a little bit of what's going on.

Eventually you may be able to hire a family counselor or a children's counselor to come in and spend special time with the children. There are all kinds of possibilities to address the issues of feelings and divorce with children.

Children can take the news and get on with the business of being a child. They will not only recover and be fine when they are eight years old, but they'll be fine when they are twenty-eight. Divorce happens to one million kids each year. Within four years, 80 percent of their parents under forty-five remarry. These changes bring new people into a child's life. Stepparenting and blended families are frequent. It is not just ties to parents that are left and remade; ties to grandparents, friends, aunts, uncles, and other relatives change. Through all of this, children can sail confidently if their self-esteem is powered with love that is expressed frequently.

Living so much in the present as they do, kids don't know that time makes things better. Reassure them that change happens and that happiness—like summer vacations and holidays—returns in time.

Giving Children Coping Skills

Divorce is all about loss and grief. To come through a divorce intact and resilient has the potential of learning skills that remain invaluable all through life. Life has many twists and turns that bring about grief and loss. Many children who have been through divorce learn these skills of resilience at an early age. One of the reasons you want to keep children informed and involved in the divorce process is so that they do not hang on to a false hope that the parents will come back together again. Facing the reality of the situation, surviving it, and ultimately thriving again is the best coping skill a child can develop.

All loss contains the following stages, taken from Elizabeth Kubler-Ross and her great work on grief and loss: Grief Cycle—denial, anger, bargaining, depression, and acceptance. Over time, both parents and children will find acceptance of the new situation. Some of the specific coping skills children can be taught to develop are:

- *Knowing how to use support and comfort.* You can go for a walk and talk, go shopping for a special stuffed animal the child can sleep with and talk to, help them make a collage of his or her feelings, set a regular time he or she can call the other parent, or introduce a new activity in the child's life that is comforting (class, game, sport, or skill).
- *Share feelings.* Talk to the child in "feeling" words, like, "I feel sad today because things are different. I think I will read a special book and see if I can feel better. How do you feel and what would you like to do?" Another example: "Sometimes I feel lonely without Dad here. I think I will call Nancy and see if she would like to go for a walk. If you are lonely today, would you like to call a friend to come and play?" This kind of talk addresses the reality and also offers a solution at the same time.
- *Anticipate trigger times.* It is very important to know that holidays, birthdays, and vacations are going to be trigger times. It is good to anticipate these times and make them as meaningful as possible. Making sure that holidays are something to be savored and enjoyed contributes a great deal to resiliency. At these times, it becomes necessary for each

parent to do whatever he or she can to make the child's life as happy as can be under the present circumstances.

- **Consider a pet.** If your child has a pet, this is a time to foster the relationship between the child and the pet. Assuming additional responsibility for the pet gives the child something to focus on. Let the pet start sleeping in the child's room if that has not been allowed before. If the child does not have a pet, this might be the perfect time to get one. Pets aid healing and they love unconditionally, especially dogs. It gives a child something to love and it loves back. However, be sure your child is ready and that the pet will be loved and cared for.
- **Implement consistency in the child's life.** When there is a minimum of change in the child's life, this allows the best chance for the child to learn resilience and coping skills that will help him or her for the rest of life. Familiarity and routine will minimize fear and anger. Try to keep schedules, transition, and visitations. Even if there is inconvenience, try to work with your ex-partner as you figure out visitation schedules.

Possible Problems to Watch For

If your child starts any new behaviors that are not in his, her, or your best interest, address the situation directly and as soon as it is clear there is a problem. These problems might include isolation, an unwillingness to share thoughts or feelings, sleep problems (too much or too little), anxiety or nervousness, school issues, difficulties or changes in friendships, etc. Behavior change indicates that something is going on and you want to be there for your child.

Special Issues

When a child is in the beginning changes, he or she might be very angry with one parent and not want to see him or her at all. Each situation is different, but it is important to put the child's needs first. If a visit is resisted by a child, see what alternatives are possible. In the case of a child not being safe with one parent because of alcohol use, nicotine use, drug abuse, or episodes of rage, it is up to the other parent to find ways to protect the child. That is a responsibility. To put the child in any kind of harm's way must be prevented.

> Being blind isn't so bad, it's losing your vision that's bad.
>
> —HELEN KELLER

In some situations a child wants to spend a concentrated period of time with the noncustodial parent. This could be a vacation, a summer, a semester, or even a full year. These arrangements need to be evaluated on a case-by-case basis and carefully thought through and worked out.

When possible, it is most helpful when parents can agree on boundaries, discipline, bedtime, rules, homework, friends, etc. Ultimately, this works best for the child in the long run. Rarely do parents agree on everything, but the more things they can agree on, the safer the child feels.

Secret Thoughts Not Always Shared by the Child
- I really want both of you in my life. I know it can't be like it has always been, but I need to know you are there with me.
- Please don't talk bad about my other parent. I am their child, too. If I am anything like them, does that mean you wish you could divorce me, too?
- I hurt when you talk bad about my other parent.
- Please call me, write me, and ask me questions. I need to know that I am important to you.
- Please don't ask me to carry messages. I am a child, not your message carrier.
- Please don't expect me to take sides. This is all hard enough for me.

- Tell me you love me many times. I need to hear it even if I roll my eyes and look embarrassed.
- Listen to me and listen to the meaning behind my words and my actions. Sometimes I don't say things right, but I am doing the best I can.
- Be patient with me. I am trying to adjust to all the changes at the same time I am trying to grow up and trying to give you a message.
- Take care of yourself and find your own happiness. I can't be everything for you. It's too much.
- Try to stay happy. My life has enough sorrow right now. Worrying about you is something I can't handle right now.

It is important to keep the love flowing. No child ever had too many hugs, too many smiles, or too much affection. Yet this loving approach does not do well when one parent buys the child too much in order to replace love. Buying does not work well in the long run for a variety of reasons.

Changes of any kind are hard—but divorce is one of the hardest. Know that with knowledge, willingness on the part of the parents, and courage to follow through, it does not have to be a devastating change for the children. It can even be a positive change. If you and your former spouse will work together and communicate what is the best for the young child, the original family unit can become an important family unit for all time—incorporating the stepfamily aspects.

The deeper the sorrow carves into our soul,
the more joy we can someday contain. There is hope.

ANITA RAFFLE

PARENTAL COOPERATION

Some of the inevitable changes and events in the lives of children will help heal the problems associated with divorce. Both parents very likely will want to be present, harmoniously, for children at graduations, school programs, weddings, births, baptisms, and bas and bar mitzvahs. Each of these times provides an opportunity for parents to show their children that they want to support and honor them. Their presence says that what went on between the parents is private, between them, but each parent will continue to be there for the child. This kind of cooperation in itself is healing for children. If the parents are willing to make some of these concessions, independence and maturity can be strengthened for the children by watching their divorced parents.

Parenting tends to be for life, even though marriages aren't always.

In addition to hearing that both parents will never stop loving them, children need to know that there will be continuous interaction for years, and that both parents are committed to their emotional and financial well-being.

Divorced parents will be required at many different times and in different ways to talk to each other and negotiate again. If they can keep open lines of communication, share parental decisions, and retain an appropriate level of respect, they will minimize the effects of divorce on the children. Sometimes we are so estranged from our ex-spouses that we need a third party available at all discussions about our children. Sometimes we can learn to negotiate together reasonably, but a counselor may be able to help us do it more easily. Whatever difficulties we might have, they will work out best if they are brought out on the table and if negotiated solutions are regarded as binding by both parties.

Often, because of my work, I spend a great deal of time traveling and in airports. There I frequently see a painful picture of the younger children of divorce trudging along, hand in a parent's, carrying their duffle bags of commuting toys and clothes to one of their two homes. These children know that in one house the plates are on high shelves and in the other house the plates are on low shelves. In one place they have a bed of their own, and in another they may share a bed with a sibling. For these transient youngsters, life is like learning to live with constant culture shock as they travel between two "foreign countries," with different "languages," different rules, different expectations, and different lifestyles. Sometimes these children go through unnecessary suffering because the parents, in their own pain, often don't see the needs of their children.

For commuting children of divorced parents, travel is no vacation. Adjusting to the different cultures of their two homes can be stressful. Parents need to acknowledge the children's situation, encouraging and praising their flexibility, which will aid them later in adulthood.

Parental cooperation can ease the trials of children who must change homes periodically. Parents need to be aware of the difficulty in shifting to a different order and remember their child's age and stage of development.

Separating Fact from Fantasy

When past relationships within the family have been painful, we may come away with bitterness; however, when we dwell on how our families were happy or were perceived to be happy, we can develop unreal fantasies as we idealize the past. We might choose to remember that our lives were always about vacations, such as Disney World, and good food on the table. In fact, the parents may have tilted appearances one way or the other, but the truth was quite different.

Parents can help children remember that there were both good things and painful things about the past—and there will be some good things and some hurtful things about the future.

DON'T PUT MESSAGES IN MONEY

Often money becomes tighter as people need to change their lifestyles. Sometimes money gets easier. What is significant is that money should not be used with children to demonstrate approval or punishment. The parent with the most money may try to buy the children's devotion, loyalty, and love. Disconnect these emotions from dollar signs in your children's eyes at every opportunity.

LOYALTY

In crises and stress, children may feel a lot of shame about what is happening with their parents. Often they feel a strong sense of loyalty toward one or both. When they are being pulled both ways, sometimes they find the only person they can talk to is a therapist. In therapy children often realize for the first time that what they are feeling is anger and hurt. If their loyalty to their parents is acted out at the children's expense, they may need to learn to love themselves enough to say no to painful conflicts.

SHARING AND STRETCHING SPECIAL DATES

As visits, holidays, and times with each parent are worked out, children should be kept out of listening range. They can be made to feel like bartered objects. There are many optional ways of dealing with this. Some people have Christmas on a different date. Some celebrate birthdays one year with one family, one year with the next. Each of the children can have some vacation time with each parent. Insisting on the observance of a special event on a conflicting date isn't nearly as important to a child as not being the subject of discord between their parents.

CHILDHOOD CHALLENGES OF DIVORCE CAN BENEFIT ADULTHOOD

Some behavioral experts think the adversity of divorce, with its challenges, actually has a positive effect on children, and that some of them end up being wiser and learning more about love because they have suffered loss. Perhaps they may even turn out more creative. According to *Business Week*.

Creative people usually don't have dull, predictable childhoods. Instead, childhood is marked by exposure to diversity. Strains in family life, financial ups and downs, or divorces are common. Experts believe a dose of diversity gives children the ability to see issues and problems from different points of view. Creative types are generally independent and highly motivated. They are also great skeptics, risk takers and thinkers. Disorder does not make them anxious. Indeed, they relish it.[1]

> Be gentle with yourself and your children. They, too, are experiencing trauma and need understanding support. Divorce presents a special opportunity for increased bonding with children.

YOUNGSTERS AREN'T ALWAYS DISTURBED BY DIVORCE

Leading up to many divorces are times of "cold war," "the silent treatment," loud, dish-throwing fights, sometimes physical violence, and sometimes pure silent abandonment. Children feel what is going on, whether it is directed at them or not, and whether or not they are brought into the prime action.

Often divorce is a relief that can lessen anxieties and remove uncomfortable or scary feelings. Children will become much less nervous in an atmosphere of peace and less likely to seek too much diversion outside the home.

KIDS WITH TWO HOMES OFTEN BENEFIT

The ideal situation is to live full-time in one home, but consider other possibilities as equally beneficial:

1. If children have contact with two parents, they have a sense of security in two places, rather than just one. They also have a broader perspective about life and realize there is not just one way of looking at things. They are exposed to more than one set of values and have an opportunity to combine and create their own.

2. The two homes may offer an expanded network of support. At each home there may be a different set of relatives who now show up, new neighbors, and children to play with. Two home sites may have many more options than one.

      Whether a family remains intact in a first marriage, whether it becomes modified into a single-parent family, or whether a remarried blended family becomes the home, Virginia Satir states the classic truth. "In unhealthy families, children are there to meet the needs of their parents, to entertain, serve or glorify. In healthy families, parents are there to meet the essential needs of their children, physically and emotionally."

Some Signs of Success in Divorced Homes with Happy Kids

1. Children are encouraged to form their own nonbiased opinions of all parents and stepparents. Parents neither sugarcoat nor blame the other parent.
2. Parents encourage expression of anger, hurt, loneliness, fears, and tears from the children.
3. Scheduling conflicts are handled by parents, and children are not put in the middle of the stress and strain.
4. Children have role models of happy relationships. Each parent either provides this with a new partner or spends time with the kids and other families where these relationships exist.
5. Each parent affirms each child's self-worth as often as possible to reinforce the reality that divorce ends a marriage not the parent-child bond. Children of all ages need to hear:
   - I'm glad you are my son/daughter.
   - You are special.
   - I like spending time with you.
   - I love you.
6. Parents keep good boundaries about their own divorce concerns. Many family therapists believe that 80 percent of parents' personal business is none of the children's business. Too often children will take on responsibility for what they know. Most of a parent's stress and conflict does not need to be known by the child.
7. Parents don't try to do everything for their children. Children do not need superparents. This only causes inadequacy and role modeling that creates anxiety.
8. Parents keep a sense of humor. Children need help in knowing there are at least two sides to everything. They need help to develop their sense of humor and to "lighten up." Seeing that their parents can be happy, whether single, or post-divorce, is an inspiration.

As Children Mature

Parents are to parent children; children are to be children.

Many situations will require special negotiation and consideration as children grow up. In a healthy family, parents and children take the time and attention to work these out to the best advantage for each person involved. In a healthy family, compromise and negotiations become an important part of day-to-day living. In a painful family, situations become opportunities for control and power struggles. More emphasis is on winning and being right than on finding solutions.

Painful and Healthy Family Relationships

Painful	Healthy
Major focus on one member.	All are heard and considered.
Children are expected to meet the needs of the parent.	Parents are expected to meet the needs of the children.
Lots of secrets.	Openness and honesty.
Parents tell children how to live.	Parents show children how to live.
Everyone in the family is involved in the business of the other.	Each family member is given space and privacy with respectful boundaries.
There is loyalty to each family member, even if not deserved.	Member are able to choose how or whether to stay actively related.

Painful and Healthy Family Relationships (cont'd)

Painful	Healthy
Shame-based people, low self-worth in each family member.	Mistakes, making up, and forgiveness are taught and accepted.
Gloom and frequent depression or sadness prevent a happy family atmosphere.	The family has a good time together, with joy, a sense of humor, and laughter.

Flexibility

As families mature, many more changes will be needed in keeping with the times. Riding with these changes makes life easier for both you and the children. Several areas in which adjustments will be made over the years are:

1. *Money management.* As mentioned earlier, sometimes there is less money available following a divorce. Some suggestions in regard to finances: One or both parents provide the necessities for the children (housing, medical care, food, daily support); then for larger purchases (braces, graduation, wedding expenses, car insurance, trips), both parents contribute. Later on the child can become an additional contributor. Realizing the amount of negotiation and interaction that will continue long after the divorce, parents should try to maintain as much ability to communicate with each other as possible from the start.

2. *Feelings will go up and down.* Riding an emotional roller coaster is normal. The more children talk about all the feelings they have, the easier it will be to let go of the feelings that they don't want. These feelings include:

• ANGER . . .
At the parent who started the divorce
At the parent who leaves
At the parent who stays

• FEAR . . .
Of needing to move and sometimes change schools.
Of what other kids will say
Of needing to take care of a parent
Of parents no longer loving them
Of not enough money
Of losing a parent

• GUILT . . .
Over having contributed to the divorce

• SADNESS . . .
Over losing access to grandparents
Over losing two-parent family vacations

Depression, rage, or hysteria in children can be the result of inadequately expressed feelings that build over time. Children should be encouraged that feeling angry is natural and that it's all right to cry. During a divorce, it's normal to have feelings of hurt, sadness, and loss. They need to be told that it's important to express emotions and to express them when they are first felt.

With very young children, sometimes sharing feelings can be done in the context of telling or reading a story and reflecting on the feelings. Even before children are able to read or write, they are able to draw pictures—another way for children to express their feelings. Later, as soon as youngsters are old enough to read, help them pick out books about divorce at the library or bookstore. Look for magazine articles with items about divorce. It makes children feel better to know they aren't the only ones going through this experience.

Checking with your children's school may reassure you that there are resource people and support groups for children of divorce. If the school doesn't have these services, you may want to start one. Perhaps your house could be the place where the children could gather. The get-together can be leaderless, with children simply talking about the difficulties they are facing. Or you might want to plan some group activities to help them release the stresses of divorce.

3. *Child custody battles have no winners.* Regardless of how we might like it to be, if children are involved in a divorce, blood ties are going to last forever, way beyond the end of child support at eighteen. When a child gets married, that's a family affair. When the first child is born to your child and you and your ex-spouse now have to share grandchildren, that's a family affair. When there is a terminal illness, a crisis, or a trauma in the lives of one or the other parent, that is a family affair. The luckiest children will be those who are allowed to have whatever experiences they need to have with either parent, without interference or criticism. A wonderful book to help parents struggling with custody issues is *Divorced Families: Meeting the Challenge of Divorce and Remarriage* by Constance B. Ahrons, PhD.

4. *Changing rituals and relationships.* Meals, exercise, friendships, guests in the house, school events—any of these daily encounters may have to be renegotiated with our children. Some rituals, such as holidays and vacations, may have to be scaled down or the dates altered, but only the positives should be emphasized.

Painful Times for Families

In my divorce survey, parents uniformly agreed that Thanksgiving, Christmas, and Hanukkah were highly stressful and possibly painful times for families. Holidays tend to bring out the best and worst in relationships.

Be prepared to handle your children's nostalgic emotions that may arise during holidays. Following are some ways to deal with these emotional incidents.

THANKSGIVING

This holiday signals the beginning of a season that can bring sadness as well as joy to divorced families. It's a time for nostalgia, when many of us reflect on the good times we used to have as a family. The rituals we observe on this holiday provide us with a sense of continuity year after year. Families come together and share turkey, dressing, cranberry sauce, sweet potatoes, pumpkin pie—all of our traditional holiday foods.

But all things change, and Thanksgiving is no exception. It was once a time when the food brought to the table was hunted by the men and grown in home gardens by the family. It was a time when families ground their own grain, pressed apples for cider, and made their own butter. As that era has passed, so has another. We can commemorate the old times, but we can also update Thanksgiving and make it a holiday tradition much more focused on the present and the future.

Adopting and adapting are happening everywhere today with the Thanksgiving meal. A light salad and fresh vegetables may replace some of the traditional items, and rich desserts may be substituted with low-cal ones, such as a pumpkin soufflé. We can even take the entire event and make it a celebration with new habits. Rather than everyone sitting around watching football after dinner, everyone could go to the fitness club or take a long leisurely walk together, reflecting on what the year has brought.

Figure 11.1. Holidays

As we sit around a different-looking holiday table, we could talk about changes with our children: How there is more than one breadwinner in a family now, how we have the convenience of microwaves and ovens for quick and easy baking, and how other convenience foods (well-loved by children) have changed our lifestyles from those of previous times.

And by the way, a reality check may be in order. Perhaps the history of holiday time wasn't as rosy as we long to remember it. Were there tensions that nobody wanted to talk about? Unspoken feelings always hanging in the air? As we try to improve our lives through this process of divorce, we may take this holiday and move forward with it, knowing we are celebrating in harmony, with all of us wanting to be there. We can be free with feelings and thoughts, and the self-worth of each person will be honored. Let's go for a lighter meal, a lighter touch, and lots of love.

Our harvest is in. We have a lot to be thankful for.

CHRISTMAS AND HANUKKAH

These are the Big Ones. Throughout our family life together, all of our Christmases are supposed to be "bright," just as the song says. You might not make it home for Thanksgiving, but Christmas and Hanukkah are definitely watersheds of family feelings. Because people's memories tumble back one way or another at this time of year, the season is loaded with bygones, personal histories, and sometimes myths. Any holiday has a hard time living up to our expectations. Is it any wonder that during the holiday season the suicide rate and hospital admissions for depression are so high? Realism and idealism collide on the day after, and many people are left saying, "Is that all there is?"

Holidays will continue to be fun if families allow themselves to remake traditions.

When we have gone through a divorce or our family has become a divorced family, it's to our advantage to plan ahead for these delicate days. First, you may need to revise the calendar. When children are to be shared during the season, get the whole family into the mood of flexible fun. For example, there is nothing that you do on December 25 that can't be done on some other day. You can easily work out which weekend in December will be holiday-celebration time for which group of relatives.

No law says you can't have Christmas fun on the second, third, or fourth weekend in December, as well as the actual date of the twenty-fifth. In our family, celebrations have been rearranged so that we can count on Christmas coming the second weekend in December. We have had many wonderful Christmases in this way, with our very own special calendar. This leaves two more weekends, plus Christmas itself, during which we can share the spirit with other members of our extended or divorced families.

Many benefits come with choosing a date other than the conventional one. They include:

1. Smaller crowds.
2. Frequent-flyer airplane tickets can be enjoyed without having to worry about the holiday blackout dates.
3. Christmas Eve and Christmas Day are free of hectic distractions and available for reflection, relaxation, and enjoyment without pressure.
4. The opportunity to "clone" Christmas or Hanukkah. If it is so wonderful, why not celebrate it several times during the month of December?
5. A date-free holiday. Sometimes we can dispense with the whole idea of having to choose a specific date and just enjoy the entire month as it is.

Once we have selected the most positive way to schedule them, then we can begin to plan the ways we will celebrate the holidays. Emphasize the fun of the unconventional approach, of having the power to break out of the mold if the mold doesn't work anymore. There are many, many options for making what once was a predictable routine into a memorable change of pace.

I will never forget the first time we celebrated Christmas following my divorce. I simply packed the kids into my old car, my son brought along a very small artificial tree, and we had Christmas every night in a Holiday Inn on our way down to experience Disney World as a changed family. It was a very special Christmas—no presents—because we were saving our money for Disney World; however, I think that this Christmas stands out in the memories of my children as one of the best holidays they ever had.

Sometimes unusual company for Christmas puts a delightful spin on the season. I remember one Christmas we went to a local church and asked them to recommend a lonely family for us to share with. Not only did we enjoy the day but we had the good feeling of knowing that we helped somebody else have fun, too.

A good friend of mine chose a similar but different route. She took her entire family to a soup kitchen where everyone spent the day bringing small Christmas gifts to people at the shelter. They also participated in making Christmas meals for others less fortunate than themselves.

Another family I knew simply could not face their big house that had always been decorated in high Christmas style. So the week before Christmas they loaded their car and took a cross-country trip, experiencing Christmas in many little towns across the United States.

A childless divorced woman I knew dreaded the Christmas holidays. She feared the loneliness and the emptiness of days when everyone else seemed to be having family fun. About a week before one Christmas, she decided she would expand her knowledge about different spiritual beliefs. From a Sunday paper she clipped out information on the services of various denominations. She went to church dinners, church sales, church services, and church Christmas programs, and she checked out synagogues. By the time the season ended, she had made several potential new friends and found many people just like herself who were looking for something meaningful to do for the holidays. She was invited to several dinner parties and declared that year to be one of the best seasons she'd ever had. She was quite astonished that her first Christmas after her divorce could be so fulfilling and joyful. In the process, she also met a woman who became a close friend and later a vacation companion.

George was concerned about his children becoming melancholy over sad regrets as the first holiday season approached since the divorce. So he and his children decided to keep their heads busy with games. He bought Scrabble, Outburst, Trivial Pursuit, the old game Twister, Bridge for Two, and Personal Preference. These were guaranteed to occupy them happily for the four or five days over the holidays when they would be together. Each night, prizes were passed out, small gifts that diffused the memory-loaded custom of opening gifts on Christmas Eve.

They invented another twist to the season by jointly preparing a different ethnic meal each night. They had Mexican dishes, Italian dishes, and a German "festival." Everyone was surprised that their first holiday as a two-house family passed so happily and peacefully.

Traditional days for celebrating remind us that we need to be realistic about our losses. We can't suspend the grieving process just because it's Thanksgiving, Christmas, or Hanukkah. But we can add positives to it. All of us who have read the work of Elisabeth Kubler-Ross and recognize the stages of grieving have come to understand that we first have to face the loss and then the feelings about those losses, not bury them. Only then can we get busy and do something about them.

Since we know the first year following a divorce is likely to be difficult every time we approach a nostalgic date, we can allow ourselves to feel the negatives but refuse to drown in them. For a full year we have to put a special effort into remodeling each holiday to disarm traditional flashpoints for melancholic moods. During the second year, holidays will be noticeably easier, and with each subsequent year, there will be less need to see the present in terms of the past. The ease with which we accept change will depend a great deal on how we handle that first year of grieving. So it becomes important to sit down with a calendar and review the special occasions that require a new look.

In addition to national holidays, each family has its own unique celebrations and annual events that need to be addressed. Maybe it's a special time of the year we spent with grandparents or an aunt. Perhaps it's the first trip to the beach at the beginning of summer or maybe the opening of ski season. If a child is graduating from school, one of the children from the family is getting married, or even an annual garage sale that was the focus of family fun, you may want to invent ways to alter the occasion, making it newer in feeling. This doesn't mean you'll have to be "Special Events Director" for the rest of your life—just for the first year for both you and the children. After that, adjustments to each of these occasions will be seen as fun, and the present will most likely be perceived as having more interesting possibilities than the past.

Many studies have shown that families that carry on traditions and routines but adjust them to a changing lifestyle are much better off when patterns in life are interrupted.

Positives for Kids with Divorced Parents

Professionals who work with families and children aren't really sure whether the difficulties experienced by children of divorce come from the divorce itself or from the years of struggle within the family subsequent to divorce. While undeniably negative economic and social changes affect many families of divorce, there are also many ways of looking at life for children after Mom and Dad split up.

On the upside is the greater independence many children acquire.

The learning can be a very painful experience or a healthy level of increased responsibility. Either way, the child has a head start on coping and often outperforms others in adulthood because of this early training.

So here are ways of seeing negative circumstances in a positive light:

1. Children learn to be responsible for themselves.
2. Children learn some mastery over their environment.
3. Children see the value of relationships and later in life may be more willing to work on a marriage. They may learn to cherish and nurture relationships more.
4. According to one researcher, children under twelve who live with divorced mothers often do better on achievement tests and have fewer skill problems than kids in two-parent homes. No one knows exactly why this happens, but it may be that divorced moms give kids the leisure time formerly spent with spouses. Perhaps with less stress in the home, it is easier to concentrate on studies.
5. Another researcher discovered that teens living with fighting parents are one and one-half times more likely to lie, bully, and express antisocial behavior, in general, than kids of divorced parents.

> *Holidays challenge us either to live in the loss or to grow from the loss. Major changes always involve some loss but always present opportunities for positive, exciting choice making.*

6. Adults whose parents were divorced are arrested half as often as adults from intact homes. This doesn't mean they don't suffer, but this sort of information is interesting.
7. In some economic groups, children of divorced parents tend to visit more attractions such as museums, zoos,

Healthy families have nothing to do with whether there are one or two parents in them.

lakes, and beaches and are more well-traveled than intact-marriage kids. This is especially true if one parent sees the children less often and finds an outing a better springboard for conversation than watching TV. (Working Moms with custody and no or inadequate household help may hope that Dad takes charge of the excursions.)

12

DIVORCE AND
ADULT CHILDREN

Therapists and parents have concerned themselves for many years about the effects divorce has on young children. Not until recently have the effects of divorce on adult children been recognized, or how these adult children can impact the quality of the life of the divorcing parents.

Issues adult children face include many of the same issues younger children face, such as divided time between two parents, changes in financial stability, a kaleidoscope of feelings, and loss of trust and familiarity. In addition, by virtue of age and maturity, the older child faces monumental questions about trust and reality.

They lived in a home that they now question. Was any of my life in that home with those parents honest, or were they waiting for me to grow up in order to separate? What was real and what wasn't? If the divorce takes place during the college years, what will that mean? Will my parents be able to help me finish college, or will the money situation change drastically?

Adult children with children of their own wonder what the grandparenting will look like. How will holidays be handled? Is this the end of an era of a family? The questions and concerns go on and on.

Adult children and divorced parents frequently have a real need to establish boundaries. Adult children may have become enmeshed with one or both of the parents during the struggle of the marriage. Then when a divorce takes place, the adult child sometimes moves in as a surrogate partner. This is unhealthy for both child and parent.

It's never too late to have a happy childhood.

UNKNOWN

Children and their parents should set limits and boundaries in their relationships, making sure each gets their primary needs met outside the parent-child relationship. This will allow their relationships to grow into a mature friendship.

Separating partners with adult children have many more options available to them. Each has the opportunity to develop relationships with the children that do not have to include as much contact with the ex-partner. Yet there may be times when partners' paths cross: graduations, marriages, crises, and death.

A former couple has the best chance of handling these events without discord if they approach an occasion as two single people invited individually, like a sister and brother coming together because of a piece of past history. Focusing on this shared past, rather than on painful emotions as a former couple, is possible when we care enough about peace as a permanent part of our new family life.

WHAT WAS REAL AND WHAT WASN'T?

An honest talk with both parents could shed light on this question and give some relief. An adult child may want to ask each parent how long this separation has been happening or find out about the parts of family life that were real and when things started to change. They will want to ask any specific questions that parents could possibly answer. Each parent should be given the opportunity to share his or her thoughts and feelings. Very often, this is a great help.

Susan was devastated when her parents announced their divorce during her sophomore year in college. She and her mom had always felt very close, and she had very specific and wonderful memories of the safety she had always felt around her father. Were they lying about those years of her upbringing? Did she miss something? Was it all a sham?

I have never tried to block out the memories of the past,
even though some are painful. I don't understand people
who hide from their past. Everything you live through
helps to make you the person you are now.

SOPHIA LOREN, ACTRESS

When Susan talked very specifically to her mother, Nancy, she gave her mother the chance to tell her how wonderful those days were. Nancy explained that she and Susan's father were close during those days. It was only within the last year or two that she became aware that things were changing, and they had nothing to do with Susan. Their interests had changed. They were relatively young and discovered that they wanted different things in life. They were growing apart and certain events happened that meant they couldn't go on in their marriage. Susan's mother was able to assure her that the relationship was intact during her daughter's growing-up years and that Susan hadn't missed out on anything important.

Susan had the same talk with her father, Carl. She had always adored him and thought he could do no wrong. In this particular case, her father asked her to go to a therapist with him, as he had some difficult things to share. Susan and her father went together to his counselor. In the first session, Susan's father assured her that he loved her, her mother, and her brother all the years they were together. He reassured Susan that she hadn't perceived things one way when they might have been another. He told her he still loved her.

In the second session, he talked about how his life had changed quickly when he took a different position in the same company he had always worked in during Susan's growing-up years. He was challenged by the job and was assigned an assistant, Pat, to help him through his increased responsibilities. Pat was fun, helpful, and competent. They discovered that they both liked movies. During a few of their out-of-town trips, they found some rest and relaxation by going to the movies. Movies eventually led to dinners, and an intimacy was soon forged that neither one of them was looking for but happened. While Carl was gone, working on long projects, Nancy found a life for herself. She joined a book club, got very active in her church, and even went on short weekend trips with other women. Nancy even went back to school and was on her way to becoming a social worker. She felt fulfilled and pretty content. Then the inevitable happened.

Both Carl and Nancy knew they were growing apart but were in denial over how serious the separation had become. Nancy got more and more involved in school and Carl and Pat quickly became a personal and professional couple. The relationship turned sexual one night on a long three-week trip. That was it. They discovered they had grown to love each other and Carl and Nancy had little left in common. Once Nancy knew about the sexual affair, she was hurt and devastated. There was no going back. She asked Carl for a divorce.

It was at this moment that Susan was told about the divorce. A time when it was too late to impact either parent, and she was left processing information that was a done deal. She felt left out, she felt cheated, and she felt angry. She was also worried. Would Pat move into her father's life in a way that threatened Susan's finishing college? Pat was younger than Carl. She was closer to Susan's age than her mother's age. Would she use up some of the affection Carl reserved for Susan? Could she ever trust her dad again? Would she feel extra responsibility for her mother? Would she have to take care of her mother emotionally? How would they handle holidays? Would she be able to trust men in relationships?

Susan sought a therapist and began her own journey of processing all her fears and feelings. This help and the honest interactions she had with her parents will go a long way to aid her in the healing process. She is a step ahead in knowing that she needs professional assistance. Susan's prognosis is good.

> Promise me you'll always remember:
> You're braver than you believe, and stronger
> than you seem, and smarter than you think.
>
> CHRISTOPHER ROBIN TO POOH

Financial Concerns

Financial concerns are very real. When you have a one-salary family, these concerns tend to be even greater. It means one salary has to pay for two households. Should the salary-contributing partner marry again, there will be even more stress as to how the money will be divided. If that partner has more children, it will need to stretch even further. Even in a situation with two salaries, rarely does the family live as well financially as they did before the divorce. There are just many more expenses as the family picture changes.

Adult children see everything that is going on. They have concerns that money will go to dad's new girlfriend or mom's new boyfriend. They feel this just isn't fair and often fail to give that person a fair chance to enter the picture. They worry that one of the parents will not be cared for and they will need to financially take care of that parent.

They often feel guilty about "doing well" themselves. Some even slip back in their own pursuits as they feel they don't deserve to move ahead in life. They avoid finishing their education, applying for good jobs, saving money, or planning for their future. They seem to experience a type of "survivor's guilt" feeling that says they don't deserve to be any happier than either of their parents. Sometimes this is a conscious thought. At other times, it is very subtle and they don't know why they are so unmotivated.

> When making a decision, ask yourself if this is the kindest thing you can do for yourself. Then make your decision.
>
> MAGGIE DOWAL

They concern themselves with wills and trusts and feel that second spouses and sometimes second families will take what belongs to them. To first families, there are some tips and tools to work with:

- *Look at helping the neediest parent.* I don't mean financial help. Do not take away the responsibility of the parent who needs help, but do offer support and encouragement for the parent to make their own way. Encourage the parent to go to school and get a job. If he or she finds a job that is very meaningful, it might be a whole new way of life. If an appropriate job can't be found, encourage the parent to get a job simply to make money and use any spare time to volunteer so there is a feeling of purpose in life. Nothing is more self-damaging than doing nothing but complaining about a financial change in one's life. That stance is usually full of blame and self-pity.
- *Take care of yourself without guilt.* Do not neglect your own way of walking through the world. You are your responsibility and chairman of your own board. Take time for your own relationships, finish your education, get whatever job you want wherever you want to get it. You are not responsible to fix the life of either parent. You have the right to take care of yourself. The truth is you stand a good chance of losing parental support and any family inheritance.
- *Encourage your parents to investigate long term insurance.* Usually in an original family, when one family member

declines in health, the other partner is there for them.
When that partner dies, the children often step in to help
the surviving parent. When there is a divorce followed by
remarriages and stepfamilies, often several people are involved,
and care for different parents becomes a more complex issue.
Also, geography plays a big role because the parents may live
miles away from the different children. Setting up long-term
care for both parents may be a very wise move. This could
be part of a divorce agreement or settlement. Children of
divorcing parents may end up with two parents needing help in
two different cities and no one to care for either of them.

- *At the time of divorce, ask for what you need.* It may be hard to
  bring up something so material as to the goods in the divorce.
  Yet many family squabbles may have been avoided if the child
  spoke up. If there is a sentimental item that means something,
  it is okay to say to a parent, "I have always loved the pillow that
  Grandma hand stitched for you and I hope you might earmark
  it for me in the settlement or when you no longer want it
  yourself." Or maybe special dishes that were used during the
  holidays mean something to the children and they would like
  to have those earmarked as well. Countless sentimental gifts
  that might even be made at the time of divorce proceedings
  could help the healing process. This includes photo albums or
  gifts that were handmade by the children (which should always
  be given back to the child who made them). If you are that
  adult child, do not be afraid to ask for them. Tell your parents
  you cherish these items and they are important to you.
- *Make arrangements to start new traditions.* Ask for your
  parents' help in this process. Do not feel you need to spend
  the holidays running back and forth to parents in order to
  make them feel better. Maybe choose to spend one holiday
  with one parent and another with the other. Invite them to
  come see you on these holidays, or you go see them. You may

choose to see neither of them. Go on a vacation, or spend it
with friends. This is a time of compassion, understanding,
and self-care. After all, holidays are a date on a calendar
that can be celebrated at any time.

Divorce Late in Life

We see an increasing number of divorces in the over-sixty age
group. Why are people divorcing at that advanced age? There are
many reasons. One attorney friend shared with me that she had
recently handled a case of someone who was asking for a divorce at
the age of ninety-one.

Some of the issues include older men wanting to recapture youth
with a younger woman. Sometimes it is to feel younger and more
vibrant, and sometimes it's to ensure that a healthier woman is there to
take care of them in their older age. Another factor is early retirement.
They may retire early and find that they really don't know their partners.
They had been too busy in their parenting and grandparenting years to
build a closeness and mutually satisfying relationship with each other.

In this later stage in life, they find that one wants to travel and one
does not. One wants to visit the grandchildren frequently; one does
not. One wants to entertain and have a social life, the other wants to
downsize and read. One wants to stay active, the other wants a qui-
eter life. Sometimes older people divorce to enjoy their solitude and
way of life, and sometimes they want to find someone who will share
their life interests. Older people often tend to have more disposable
income and can make the changes they want to make. Another
contributing factor is that family members live distances from one
another, and the social stigma of a divorce is lessening all the time.

Unfortunately, there is a mind-set that says, "Oh well, at least the kids are okay. They are grown and a divorce now might not affect them badly." Perhaps the effect on adult children is underestimated. Yet the kids often do feel "the family is ending." They might not give the family too much thought from day-to-day, but therein lies the assumption. "The Family" will always be there for me—never changing.

Twenty years from now, you will be more disappointed by the things that you didn't do than by the ones you did do. So throw off the bowlines. Sail away from the safe harbor.

MARK TWAIN

This leads us to another subject. What happens when a partner finds a new love and tries to incorporate him or her into a family life with adult children? As with younger children, in some situations adult children embrace whomever their parents bring into the situation. They are happy that their parents have found someone to love and be loved by. Sometimes adult children experience a feeling of relief and comfort in this new partnership. They support their parents in wonderful ways.

Divorce shakes the roots of each family member's idea of what a family is, was, and should be.

However, in other situations, there may be a great deal of pain and a total nonacceptance of the new love. This change brings tension and conflict. Sometimes the rejection is quite cruel. Too many important issues are at stake, and adult children may react with control and judgment.

If some kind of truce can be called, perhaps the family will begin healing and, under the best circumstances, a polite friendship is formed. These are very difficult situations. Too often, the core feelings of jealousy and fear of abandonment cannot be resolved. The money issue remains a thorn in the side of adult children. When a new marriage occurs, the sense of financial entitlement rears its ugly head, and adult children can and do become quite self-protecting.

Figure 12.1. The Middle

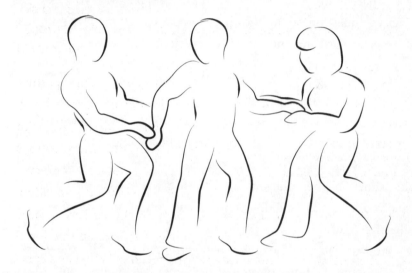

Feeling of Being Caught in the Middle

When parents have not been able to work out their differences, it is very difficult for adult children. It becomes necessary at that time for the adult child to take a stand and not take sides. It is far too easy to label one parent good and the other parent bad. You have two parents, you always will, and it is your responsibility not to label either one.

Living with the regrets of abandoning one parent or the other becomes a growing burden as time goes on. You will never have all the facts, and you will never know what each parent is going through. It is important never to be the message bearer. If one parent asks how the other one is doing, remain silent. If you say that he or she is just fine and happy, it will be upsetting. If you say that he or she is hurting, other feelings may arise. This is a no-win situation. The adult child needs to simply say, "I love you, [parent's name], but I love my other parent, too. I cannot have these discussions with you, nor will I answer questions about the other parent." Once you have said this, keep your word and end further discussions.

GIVE NEW PARTNERS A CHANCE

For the best healing of all people, give anyone involved in a new relationship with either parent a chance. Do not reject new partners or pretend they don't exist. They do and they might be bringing a great deal of happiness to your parents. Don't ever put your parents in a situation where they have to choose between their new partners and you—the adult child. It is unfair and painful for everyone. Take the high road.

Prepare yourself for any times you all need to be together—baptisms, graduations, bar mitzvahs, weddings, funerals, etc. If each family member gives a little and thinks of the feelings of the other family members, they can get along without incident.

GIVE UP UNFAIR EXPECTATIONS

Expecting the divorcing parents to dance together during a wedding dance or leaving the new partner out of wedding photos and flower corsages are recipes for disaster. Give up unfair expectations, and if everyone can be in the same room together, be satisfied that it is enough. Work with how things are rather than how you wish they could be.

CHOOSE WHAT IS IMPORTANT AND WHAT IS NOT

If it's a wedding, you might want to invite your parents. If you suffer a major loss and there is a funeral to attend, or if it is a graduation ceremony, you might want both parents to be there. These events should be attended by both your parents and the new partners. However, if it is a holiday, birthday, or some other event, it is probably best to find a way to celebrate with each parent separately.

It is best to leave the role of the "injured adult child" behind and show evidence of growing up and maturity. Children can do this when they realize that they had many of the parents' best years and they are now creating their own adulthood. Feeling gratitude for what they did have and not what has changed goes a long way toward healing. They cannot solve or change their parents' problems or situations. They can only be responsible for how they react at this current time.

> Life is no brief candle to me. It is a sort of
> splendid torch . . . and I want to make it burn
> as brightly as possible before handing it
> on to future generations.
> GEORGE BERNARD SHAW

13

THE FAMILY SYSTEM

*T*wo-parent families like to think they have a much better edge over divorced parents at producing well-adjusted children, but the facts show that Mom and Dad remaining together can do just as much damage as good. Children's emotional health is formulated by what they learn about themselves and life from the attitude(s) and lifestyle(s) of their primary caregivers(s), whether it is one person or two.

Following are some characteristics of painful versus healthy family systems, discussed at length in my book *Choicemaking*.[1] From these lists you can see that viewing good parenting in terms of the number of parents is a far cry from what actually goes into building a happy, secure home and a strong sense of self-worth in a child.

Painful Family Systems

That Lower Self-Worth Have . . .

A no-talk rule
Internalized feelings
Unspoken expectations
Entangled relationships
Manipulation and control
A chaotic value sytems
Rigid attitudes
Static traditions

Healthy Family Systems

That Build Self-Worth Have . . .

Open communication
Openly expressed feelings
Explicit rules
Respect for individuality
Freedom that is valued
A consistent value system
Open-mindedness
Flexible traditions

Obviously, painful families promote inadequacy in their family members: Families with two parents in which the father is an alcoholic frighten and intimidate their children; two-parent families where anger and hatred explode into physical and emotional abuse, sometimes with no intervention by the passive partner; two-parent families in which no one trusts the other, and lying and cheating are normal and expected; families where one or both of the parents spend so much time away from home that their children couldn't possibly develop emotional security, friendships, or a sense of belonging. Often very troubled families think they are giving their children a decent home.

Then there are the families where there is peace, unity, respect, and interest in one another. These homes are safe places to live, and children feel they belong. Whether these families have one parent or two, the result of a wholesome attitude and lifestyle is the same in the children.

The main effect of a reduction of the number of parents in a family is the loss of a helpmate in task sharing. Time comes more at a premium, and children may have to reduce playtime to work together with their parent on tasks. If this task assignment is done in a spirit of facing the challenge together and making more time for Mom to do those things that children want done for them, self-esteem can be enhanced, along with a sense of belonging and sharing in a safe and nurturing environment.

How Our Family System Developed

People develop communication patterns that tend to protect their self-worth. We seek whatever pattern of communication best protects us in our system in terms of the personality we begin to develop. People learn their survival patterns in the families

> *The messages in a troubled home are not clear. A divorce is clear and children can recover from it. Positively invite them to be new homebuilders with you.*

from which they come. They take this learning with them in choosing their mates and in raising their own children.

Many things are a matter of choice, but many aren't. The educational system today has an elaborate set of schedules, learning techniques, and experiences, which are enforced on students. The hope is that the student will learn to make "free" choices independently, yet that freedom has already been curbed to some extent by nonchosen circumstances. When and where we are born, and which parents we are born to, are not matters of choice. A person enters the world "already begun," a unique personality, yet needing to belong and needing to survive physically and emotionally. Maturity brings a shift from the yearning to be included to the desire to state, "I belong." While we do "our thing" and live in a certain way, we enjoy the discovery that we are important just for ourselves. The shift to one's "I-ness" is the process of growing self-worth. As the poet Max Ehrmann says in "Desiderata," "You have a right to be here." A person in any family needs to be able to say, "I am important just because I am."

As we let go of our fantasies of "happily ever after" and the myth of being a "perfect" family, we prepare ourselves and our children for meaningful partnerships and relationships in the "real" world.

You can build this kind of family system and self-esteem among children on a daily basis, regardless of the number of parents in your family.

DEVELOPING A NEW FAMILY SYSTEM

How do you create a new way of doing things following a divorce? When healthy families communicate, people pick up on nonverbal messages and ask questions. Clichés, such as "Yes, dear, that's very nice," are nonexistent. Often family members who are overly polite with one another are very troubled. But a post-divorce family that is trying to learn how to communicate will listen very carefully to one another. Even difficult emotions such as anger will be allowed. Anger will be aired rather than allowed to fester.

In times of need, recovering families will be able to show what they are made of. They will be there for one another; no one has to be the sole hurting one. Everyone will be treated in the same way.

One characteristic of strong families—whether they're one- or two-parent—is to face problems early and be willing to solve them. Weaker families try to deny that problems exist or get into long battles over them, with accusations and blame. Their problems are not resolved and they only get worse.

When healthy families try to discuss problems, the focus remains on finding solutions. Painful families tend to focus on assigning blame. The ability to negotiate and compromise is the most important hallmark of a family. It is healthy to encourage your children to have different hobbies and sports and to like various foods, restaurants, and movies. This kind of different energy can sometimes be celebrated by bringing the whole family together on a Friday or Saturday night and prompting everyone to share what has been meaningful to them that week.

Two important dynamics occur when difference is promoted: First is that each child is validated for the beliefs, interests, and styles he or she has, and second, everyone will learn from one another. This keeps a family energized and strong with each other.

A Solid Family Core

All families, but especially divorced families, need to find a solidifying core that holds them together. In days gone by, very often that core was the nucleus of Mom and Dad. Sometimes it was a church. Today, as things have changed for many people, this core needs to be some kind of a value system. I know of one family in which the only factor that holds them together is the belief in individual respect for each person. Today, twelve years after divorce, the members still come together frequently. Even though the children are grown, the family meets four or five times a year because they know it is the one place, the one unit, and the one group of people they can count on to respect their dignity, regardless of their accomplishments. They are always able to go home and receive validation for just being themselves.

Here is a list of ways to make a recovering, divorced family solid:

1. *Express appreciation often.* Look for opportunities to praise one another sincerely rather than pointing out annoyances.

2. *Ask the children to name the three favorite phrases they like hearing from the family.* Hopefully, they will be things like "I love you," "You can stay up late," "Yes, we'll order pizza," "Yes, we'll go to the beach [lake, mountains . . .]." Be aware that all families share some common pleasures and that supportive messages are important to them.

3. *Build the self-worth and self-esteem of every family member every opportunity you get.* It is so easy to tear esteem down and so hard to encourage it.

4. *Promote different values among family members, such as different musical tastes, different hairstyles, different attitudes and senses of humor.* Not only will this lessen the competition in the family, but it will bring members together to share their uniqueness and gain respect and honor for their differences. Differences, strangely enough, can become the core that holds the family together.

5. *Teach everybody listening skills.* At the family gatherings, every member needs a chance to talk for ten full minutes

with no comment. During this time, everyone can count on being heard without interruptions. Afterward, you might want to close your eyes, take it all in, and then let the discussion go wherever it may.

6. ***Don't duck family problems.*** Face them with acknowledgment of feelings. Pull together the family members who have a problem. Allow each person a certain amount of time to share their feelings and their position. If the problem can be resolved, do it. If not, let it sit for a few days and try again. Don't be afraid to seek outside help if you need it. Professionals are around who can quickly help the family overcome the bumps of communication. Seeking advice sooner, rather than later, will help resolve the conflict with more ease and less pain a whole lot faster.

THE ORGANISM OF A FAMILY

A family is an organism with parts interdependent on one another. Its members operate in a system, as a productive whole whose parts work together for the common good. This system has a variety of goals: peace and harmony, efficiency and survival.

A family also resembles a mobile, one of those art forms made of rods and string. Different shapes are hung on each piece of string. The beauty of the mobile is in its balance and movement. The mobile has a way of responding to changing circumstances like the wind or the touch of a hand. The mobile changes position but always maintains balance. The whole system moves interdependently to maintain its equilibrium.

The benefit of the mobile is that even though the location of each part varies, that part still has its place and importance in the balance of the whole system, even when the shape changes. The mobile's movement toward balance is similar to a family's. As members go through life, families face the stressful circumstances of a new arrival, a tragic accident, an announcement of a serious illness, or loss of a job. In response, family members shift to maintain equilibrium for peace, stability, and survival.

A family system that works efficiently and effectively depends upon three factors:

1. Each family member must have an awareness of his or her worth and importance to the family.
2. The rules of living together support each other's self-worth with respect.
3. Each family member must communicate congruently— consistently and honestly with himself and others.

In families of low self-worth, the members' fears and secrecies become paralyzing ingredients of the family stress. The members react to external behaviors rather than respond to people. The goal of a dysfunctional family is not the nurturing of the members toward self-worth. In contrast, the goal is to rigidly maintain the pretense of family balance so that their identities as "wife," "husband," and "children of . . . " remain undisturbed.

Life-Affirming Attitudes

With the confidence that is built on a peaceful family foundation, you and your children can center on life-affirming attitudes, such as the following:

- Having realistic expectations of yourselves and others
- Appreciating your efforts and enjoying the support and compliments you receive

- Taking some time each week for yourself, doing something that's important to you
- Letting some events develop without controlling each move
- Becoming increasingly aware of how you feel, and responding to those feelings
- Affirming and appreciating those around you
- Expecting wonderful things to happen to your children and you
- Becoming increasingly proactive

Children can be shown that change is natural and not to be feared. In nature, we can observe that each season gives way to the next. Our children can learn to trust the changes in their lives and to observe that as one door closes, another opens.

14
A NEW YOU
FOR A NEW LIFE

Joan: When there's alcohol in the family you grew up in, life is strange and you adjust. But that maladjustment can stay with you into a marriage, where it does not make any sense and causes trouble. When I was a child, if I heard doors slam and furniture fall heavily to the floor, or if I found my mother in tears on the couch, I pretended not to see or hear. The next morning life would go on as if nothing had happened.

I learned not to say anything and I learned to worry. I was always trying to do what I could to help and at the same time feeling guilty for being a burden. I was angry because the other kids at school seemed so secure. I cried myself to sleep, but I never told anyone. Daylight hours were for making people happy. These reactions, year after year, became the way I behaved when I had problems with people. I never thought about how these responses started or that everyone didn't react as I did. To me this is what being a person was. However, this way of dealing with life didn't help my marriage.

Each time I went home, my father cried and told me how much he loved me. After my first child was born, we went home to visit but had a horrible time. I could tell my father was drinking constantly. He didn't look or act drunk, but he had that familiar glassy-eyed, vacant look. For my own sanity, I had to leave sooner than my parents expected. I knew the only way would be to slip out with the baby at night. But my father caught me and said that if I left, I'd never be welcome again.

Later, whenever my parents called, I ran to them. But it seemed as if I could never make things right between them or for them. I felt perpetually inadequate as I tried to help them, but the alternative was to feel even more guilty for not being there. Their house was deteriorating, just like their lives, and I wanted to get involved in fixing it up. My husband objected and said my energy should be spent in our home with our children.

Then my parents started getting sick, first one then the other. I would drive the fifty miles to their home and rush back to take care of my own family. It was taking too much out of me. I was afraid my mother would die or that my children would get hurt while I was gone. I was worried I might get ill and "who would take care of everyone then?"

As my husband tried to calm me down, I made him feel helpless. Nothing he could say would make the guilt or the worry about my parents go away. I finally just collapsed, useful to no one.

Part of my process of change included professional counseling. It felt good to have someone hear how I felt and to be reassured I was a good person. I became able to separate my behavior from who I was, and to separate the disease of my parents from the people my parents were. That's when I began to love and respect myself in a new way. It was hard and it took time, but it happened.

How could we have made such a mistake? Why did we let "it" happen? What made us hang in there so long?

Maybe some of these questions have dogged you as you've thought about the past. Also, what about the future? How can we possibly avoid future hazardous relationships when we didn't predict the crash of the last one? Maybe we're stumped over why we held on so long to a marriage that obviously wasn't made in heaven.

Then there's what may seem to be the "Big Black Hole of Singlehood" looming ahead. Maybe we're anticipating major loneliness. Perhaps we've never really lived alone for long or were never good at it. Now we're by ourselves again and we wonder how Sally or Jim can stand living alone. What does it take not to go bananas, being the only adult in the house?

Exploring the Past

"What's wrong with me that this divorce happened (or this marriage happened at all)?" and "How can I keep from feeling down about being by myself?" After a marriage ends, these two sets of self-doubts are to be expected. The more you explore these doubts, rather than trying to bury them, the stronger you will emerge from post-divorce recovery.

The sooner you figure out your stumbling blocks, the better all your future relationships will be, including the all-important one: you with yourself.

Many of the painful feelings of divorce, and new efforts to avoid past mistakes, are complicated by deeply embedded programming coming from our own families—our families of origin. A lot of us have not yet made this connection because what's not so comfortable in our relations with Mom, Dad, and family seems "normal." The glitches in our families of origin are deeply familiar and we may feel, by the time we've been married and away for some time, that we pretty much have adjusted to them. This is especially true if home is far away or one parent or both have died. However, out of sight, out of mind doesn't apply with emotional issues. If we are having prolonged adjustment and grief problems associated with divorce, and if we are concerned about not bringing old problems into new friendships, the prime suspect is our innocent maladaptation to unresolved family issues.

Before we move forward in our new divorced state, it may very well help us to go backward to the root of why we have trouble giving up choices that hurt us and why we may feel insufficient or uncomfortable alone, unable to create our own happiness.

Detaching from the old, the traditional, the safe, and the familiar can cause various emotional reactions in people, ranging from disappointment or temporary regret to sadness, depression, great hurt, or panic. Most of us find it difficult to detach from a career, an organization, an institution, or a family we felt good about. The degree of discomfort we feel clues us in to the depth of our problems with change.

If we are torn apart by our detachment and we stay that way for too long, we may need to do some inner work on our relationships with our original families. The secrets to the way we react today may lie in the history of coping with our families of origin.

What Is Family Decathexis?

Cathexis is a word taken from the Greek kathexis. It implies "holding on to a person, thing, or idea." Decathexis is the process of breaking free.

I have to thank my husband, Joseph R. Cruse, MD, for letting me incorporate some of his work into this section. He has helped many family members in their healing and growing process by introducing them to the concept of family decathexis, which is very relevant to the divorcing spouse and the changing family.

In divorce the job ahead of us is unhooking and becoming free of the ties that bind us to habitually destructive emotions and reactions. By discovering how we as children lost our free and unfettered sense of self, we will be able to reclaim the joy of an independent choice maker. We will be able to move into new areas, new relationships, and new levels of dealing with our spirituality, and improve our day-to-day living. As a result, you may find yourself way ahead of your pre-divorce self in your capacity to make good decisions, avoid harmful friends, develop abilities, and enjoy life.

It is natural when we lose our mates to feel that something is missing, that we are at a loss. Our spouses provided qualities that we may have lacked. They may have confirmed our worth by laughing at our jokes, seeking our opinion, and sometimes even acting on it. At least part of their patterns of living—from eating to recreation and maybe even religious practice—became ours. Now that's gone, and before the gap closes completely, we're going to continue hurting from the separation.

If our attachments have been extreme and intense, serving as our major drive and means of identification, we are in real trouble when we lose them. The pain of loss lasts and lasts. It may turn into bitterness, fear of intimacy, fear of experimentation. In this way, our sense of feeling worthwhile is scrambled. It is as if we have become "cathected"—fixed. Literally, we are holding on for dear life. This response is not inevitable but something that arises spontaneously from a past in which guilt and fear figured prominently.

If we are having or have always had problems in letting go of people, places, and circumstances, we must go back to our families of origin to see if that's where we learned to be dependent on circumstances for our wholeness and happiness. What about strong pressures to respond to our families' emotional needs? Were we made to feel guilty—either in a subtle or overt way—when we tried to separate or go our own way? At family reunions, do we slide into roles that don't feel good just to keep the peace? Do we have a different persona, a different way of relating to the family that doesn't feel natural and isn't like the way we are with friends?

When your behavior with family is substantially different and you feel like a kid when you go home, you should consider putting family decathexis on your agenda of important goals to strive for now that you're rebuilding your life. The process of decathexis not only realigns you in terms of reality with your family, but it brings up a latent strength from your center that gives you the power to triumph over change in your life. It marks your real entry into adulthood—a state of living most characterized by being independent, not just by being over twenty-one. You became independent of person or circumstance, capable of "making it" emotionally in this world.

Shaking the Family Tree

Maybe we've tried to perform minor surgery on your relationships with relatives, but the results were either ineffective or only partially successful. Yet what is the alternative? Most people certainly don't want to stop talking to Mom or Dad or both altogether, and it's impossible not to think about their impact on our lives from time to time. But not needing their approval, saying no when we want to, confirming in our own minds our independence through affirmative interaction with them may still be issues that we need to analyze and work on.

It's not enough just telling yourself that you're an adult and then falling in line when Mom or Dad "do their controlling thing." Your true self-appraisal is in how you allow yourself to be treated or, if your parents are no longer alive, what memories survive of your self-esteem in their presence.

Resolving the reality of your adulthood between you and your parents will go a long way toward healing the dependence and doubts about inadequacy in your post-divorce recovery process. Most of us choose to minimize the need to persistently deflect our parents' denials of our adulthood. We achieved some success in adolescence and don't want to relive that conflict or disrupt the truce we may have brought about since then. Moms are just that way, we say.

> *Decathexis from family members, and subsequently from ex-spouses, does not mean detaching from loving them. It is, however, our resigning from participation in unhealthy family needs. This act of self-confirmation will empower our divorce recovery.*

A foreign correspondent chuckled over her mother's embarrassing interference in her professional and personal life. In the story entitled "A Fool and Her Mummy," the writer spoke of her mother's yearly April Fool's Day tricks as "true art." She wrote they are "aggressive," "proud," and "express as best she can her desire for an intimate connection—which surely is love, gritty and complicated as it may be." Her mother demonstrates, "She will not be excluded from my life," says the writer. After describing some of the practical jokes her mother had played, she made a statement that parallels the feelings so many of us have had:

At this point, the reasonable reader must be wondering why I did not rage at my mother for crashing in on my professional life, for violating boundaries with impunity, for infantilizing me with my bosses. And in fact, I did rage. I did. But quietly. To myself. To my husband. Never to my mother. I was stopped there by habit, and by awe.[1]

Whatever action it takes, serious attitude adjustment with your family is a prelude to enhancing your sense of can-do emotional maturity. It may be a daunting project. The alternative is to continue hiding from the possibility that long-term dependence is at the root of your sense of insecurity in crises. Healing from this dependency comes faster if we can take a close look at the whole process of becoming part of a family, then leaving it. The understanding that results is a foundation for understanding all the comings and goings of life.

It takes action to break dependency. When dependency and parental expectations of a daughter or son become ingrained as ways to cope with family, plenty of confidence is needed to halt this response. The goal is not to change others but to act out your convictions for greater self-esteem. When we sacrifice our dignity or autonomy to keep the peace in the family, we are setting ourselves up for chronic inner conflict. In

Self-esteem cannot coexist with dependency.

essence, we are giving ourselves the message that parents should be rewarded for having "bothered" with us by being allowed to exploit their parenthood status at our expense.

Just Who Are We?

This is a good question to tackle at identity-crisis times like divorce. We come into this world alone. We go out of it alone. Even before birth, the placenta, which nourished us while our bodies were forming, was only adjacent to the wall of the womb.

In fact, most of the time we are on this planet, we are alone, at least with our own thoughts. That does not mean we need to be lonely. We remain part of the families we are from and part of the families we have created. We all have duplicate pieces of our parents in us, and we can all see duplicate fragments of ourselves in our children; however, no other combination of organs, tissues, cells, and feelings is like us in the world.

You are unique, distinct—an individual. No matter how similar your outer body looks, you are still a different conglomeration of impulses and attitudes, driven in directions that can't possibly parallel your parents' paths. When someone says, "You look just like your dad," there is a moment when you want to shout, "But I'm not him!" no matter how much you admire your dad. Part of us senses that the danger of losing our identities is a real one. So much of our learning has been molded and modeled by our parents; however, we know that we are actually separate from any other individual who has existed before or will exist after us.

As infants, we have an early and long history of dependence on others for our nurturing. But our family-of-origin's function is time limited. The family as a place for "parenting" and "childing" has a specific life span, which is meant to dissolve its hierarchy after having served its purpose. Parenting is taking on the responsibility to meet the needs of their children. "Childing" refers to simply doing the things that children are expected to do. A mother or father lion no longer wants to, or needs to, exert any authority over a former cub who is now grown to full size.

If it feels sad and difficult when you first think of claiming equality with your parents and of suspending your role in their eyes as a child, then that's your signal, even stronger, for a need to apply decathexis. To become strong enough for durable relationships and to recover more quickly from personal setbacks in the future, you will need to act out this separation. To be able to consider ourselves self-contained, self-responsible, and self-sufficient individuals, we need to expect, prepare for, and perform a determined and joyful decathexis, or freeing, from the concept of a lifetime sentence as a member of just one family.

If You've Lost Your Parents

When your first parent passed away, did you think, "Half of my parents are gone"? And when you lost the second parent, you may have realized, "I'm out here all by myself!" Regardless of your age, it often seems that the loss of the second parent results in a different feeling: Now we are totally separate. If our parents had been able to do a little better job of handing our independence to us all along, we might have reacted less like orphans and more like "There goes another great friend: my dad!"

Even if both your parents are gone, relating freely to yourself and others may be blocked by old messages of dependence. We take what we take from our families mostly because we have been caught up in the myth that they are the only reliable refuge in this world, no matter how inadequate. The reality that we can create our own refuge within, and maybe even a superior support system with friends, is a family heresy. But this is what true human maturity is about, and we find many parallels in nature. All mature creatures, both parents and offspring, go their own way, protect themselves, heal by themselves, and make their own alliances. With humans, the difference is largely due to our ability to imagine more and subsequently to fear more.

If you are having trouble trusting in your ability to recover and to live alone, don't underestimate the part played by society's conditioning toward dependence. Any guilt or sense of subservience you may still have stored in your family memory bank is a signal. Repeated challenges to your right to respond as you wish in family scenarios may have whittled down your self-esteem. Even more revealing was your coping method. Did you assert yourself but give in anyway? Did you swallow it in silence but keep coming back for more? Behavior patterns like these can be transferred to new relationships and undercut one's confidence in living alone.

"-Ing" Endings Don't Fit in Adult Life

When the time comes that parents shouldn't be "parenting" anymore, then children shouldn't be "childing" anymore. Instead of being aggressive like parenting, childing is a passive state of response that is also widespread after adulthood. However, children learn very quickly what actions are expected of them as children, and all too often this role is later expected of them as adults.

We hear the word parenting frequently, but the word childing, as it is defined in this book, has not made dictionaries yet. Why not make a verb out of the word child, too? Let's add that same -ing ending to other family words and acknowledge them as the special verbs they have become. How about son? A person who is acting as a son is "sonning." A daughter acting out the expectations of a daughter is "daughtering." Some daughters act as daughters and some sons as sons long past the ages of forty, fifty, sixty, and even into their seventies. By acting as daughters and sons, we are not referring to the freely given acts of love that one human naturally extends to any other cared-about person. We are referring to those disturbing words and acts that come as a response to an authority that should have ceased long ago.

Add the -ing ending to the word father. Now we're approaching a term longer in use, traditionally involving reproduction, period! But watch out! Here comes the blockbuster . . . mothering! This is a very common word in our society, loaded with shades of meaning, both glorious and inglorious. For the most part, it is a well-understood and sacred concept. But why haven't the terms daughtering and sonning been invented and come to be equally revered? Maybe that would be too embarrassing an admission. Mother is overburdened, encouraged by society to cling and control; children are underrecognized for the psychological burdens they bear in this unnatural scheme of things.

We will always be daughter, son, mother, and father, with histories we usually like to share; however, a verb side of our designations as relatives—the active participation in a stereotyped role that isn't natural after adulthood—needs to end for us to be free and powerful after divorce.

LETTING THE FAMILY ANCHOR SAIL

The belief that the family is the center of the universe can give us a measure of security while we're growing up and struggling to survive. Even if we grew up in a dysfunctional family, there may have been enough substance and enough need for love and connection to make us feel attached to whatever family member was available. But family attachment—which is not the same as love—after adulthood is the anchor that can't be lifted when we should be sailing away on our own.

If, instead of feeling glued into roles, children were encouraged to relate to their family members like friends after adulthood, life would feel much lighter for everyone. Imagine this conversation between a parent and child:

"Hey, one of these days, we're going to be loving adult friends and buddies. I will not parent you because you won't be a child any longer. Of course, you will always be my daughter [or son], but in addition, we'll be terrific friends with a long track record of acceptance and tolerance."

Hard to picture? Doesn't sound quite right? A little weird? If so, that's because we have accepted the job of being someone's perennial child, a situation not conducive to reinforcing our self-esteem after a confidence-breaking divorce.

A Healthy Family: Time Limited

The family—that is, a teaching, protecting unit—should be an active entity only while the child actually is lacking basic physical and social survival skills. Once children reach the age of twelve to fourteen, their ability to survive physically is fairly well in place. They probably could survive without further parenting and do, even at a younger age, in disadvantaged urban settings in developing countries. But social skills in today's complex society take longer to learn. This is a gray area in human evolution where society blurs its emotional needs with the needs of the children to develop self-confidence. At no time in life is social learning ever completely finished. Most of it is pursued long after the child leaves home.

Families need to change gears from tutors to friends as each child leaves home. To continue to chase the myth that the "teachers" and "pupils" still exist, and that much is to be owed and much to be paid is a most destructive path arresting everyone's emotional and spiritual growth. Many adult children, regardless of age and maturity, are still expected to be an active part of the family until the youngest reaches majority.

Parents are not the only ones who may desire a lifetime of parenting. Many of us as adult children still attempt to resurrect our families of origin. True inner security develops only as we abandon this need as not natural.

Family reunions are one way we may seek what we have not yet developed in ourselves. These family "reunitings" are fine if they are actually "old friends" getting together for fun. But if they are plays of parenting and childing, a place to try to get the acceptance and self-validation we can't give ourselves or find in adult friends, then they are stunting our emotional growth. Families that have truly and joyfully decathected will still have reunions, but not occasions that attempt to re-create the active family of the past. Spouses, young children, and in-laws will not be dragged to these events, only to feel shut out by boring role-playing that is not part of their lives. A healthy family get-together is not a commemoration of dependency.

Unfinished Assignment of Parenting

The vast majority of parents never feel they've finished their assignment as parents. They are threatened when their offspring head out into the world, and they may even feel guilt. Most of their self-worth may be wrapped up in parenting and they may fear abandonment. Many times we have heard parents say, "Boy, when all the kids are gone, we're going to really enjoy ourselves. Sure, we'll miss them, but . . . !" However, parents' feelings frequently don't match what they say. Underneath they are wondering about the loss of identity and status, loss of control, and loss of companionship. Adult children soon discover the concerns. The conflicted reaction of the parents is normal and is passed down from generation to generation, even if it isn't verbalized. Some of the ways these feelings and fears are expressed might be through comments like:

- "What am I going to do after you're gone?" (Said with a laugh.)
- "I've failed with that one, I guess!" (An aside to your aunt after you didn't show up for your cousin's wedding.)
- "I know you're thirty-four, but you can always get your own apartment. We will only be around a little while longer!"
- "That hairstyle doesn't suit you."

Family Demands: An Accepted Tyranny

Many families have spoken or unspoken expectations: "You're not coming home for Thanksgiving? Well, then, Mom probably won't bother making turkey and all the rest. I always looked forward to her great spread."

In the role of "second-class citizens," kids are just supposed to take this intimidation. Parents often aren't expected to consider the spouse's family or the young couple's right to start their own traditions. The unspoken focus is on "After all we've done for you. . . ." In this way, child rearing in many families seems to be regarded as a debt that is never paid off.

Here's a familiar scenario: Daughter, bags packed, heads off to college, looking as though she's ready to do all that she's dreamed of, ready to set her own agenda, mark her own calendar with new people to meet and events to attend. But wait! She's already promised to drive the 300 miles back from school next weekend so Mom and Dad won't feel abandoned. Furthermore, she'll give up some new adventures to make that grueling trip time after time, whenever the guilt rises to uncomfortable levels. Sure, she wants to see them, but it's time she saw others, did things with others, and learned about others. But there's no way Mom and Dad will discourage her visits back to the nest. She'll come back as a daughter who will jump into the process of daughtering, which means allowing herself to be mothered and fathered, advised and counseled, even after she protests it's not needed. She doesn't know how to stop the parenting without losing her parents. And she's been taught well to need parents permanently.

When she's married, the unnatural process will continue, only her husband will be drawn into it, either as a frustrated observer or in an active role, "sonning-in-law." By the time she's divorced, the parents may or may not still be on hand as havens of dependence or as voices from the past who remind her that she never quite outgrew her need for them.

Daughters who have had a similar kind of parenting will have a difficult time recognizing that this binding, bonding, and enmeshment, although normal, is not natural. Acceptance of what many daughters have to put up with indicates the lowered sense of self-esteem encouraged by family cathexis.

Sons caught in family webs have the same problem feeling strong and independent, despite outward appearances. They continue to undermine their own self-esteem by swallowing childing reminders from home such as "Support is always here if you need it," or, "Your mistakes might have been avoided by [fill in the blank with your favorite family precautions]," or, "By the way, whatever happened to that nice girl who was interested in you during your senior year?"

As long as we are unable to assert the inappropriateness of being parented at our age, we are still feeling the need to be a child. This doesn't give us the strength we need in divorce recovery and definitely puts us at a disadvantage in a new relationship. A child can handle only relationships with friends or parents, not mates. Having the needs of a child and still wanting approval from a parent, an adult is too busy swallowing those emotional fishhooks of the family of origin to feel powerful and self-sufficient. Many times the line and the reel are represented by the telephone, as it becomes the mechanism to "reel us in."

Divorced Children of Dysfunctional Families

Adults who were raised in alcoholic or otherwise dysfunctional families face the same difficulties of those raised in "normal" families. But they have increased problems with trying to establish significant relationships, career paths, and a life pattern that embodies self-worth. When we come from a family that is suppressed and emotionally dead, we don't deca-thect. We stay cathected. Instead of a separation into marriage or career, we simply part for a time. Then we go back and continue to try to fix up, console, support, and be physically and emotionally vigilant and "on call."

If we're from one of these highly dysfunctional families, woe to the partner we chose. Usually our whole family is only too glad to incor-porate themselves into our marriage, as if that had been the plan all along. A partner may have to fit into a set of rules, standards, and tra-ditions that can be quite rigid, especially for a new relationship that has just begun. When spouses find their beds must be shared with painful and unhealed family injuries, scars, complicated negotiations, power battles, and "responsibilities," the marriage often becomes strained. This is because neither parents nor adult children could step off the societal "sad-go-round" to grab that golden ring of independence.

Most often, people from dysfunc-tional families are attracted to potential partners who are also from families with serious problems. They have a lot to talk about. So it isn't just one spouse who will have to struggle with a "foreign" set of rules, but two. This is double trouble for a marriage or relationship. When we have such an entourage with us, we find that we are seldom able to join in the life of someone we may meet who is full of choices, free, and growing. Each day holds the excitement of free choice and positive self-regard for a "former child," without the encumbrances of a "cathetic family."

Declarations of independence aren't negations of love. Ex-spouses in divorce recovery may need to affirm their own powers by actively rejecting parents' traditional rights to emotional dependence.

THE REALITIES OF PERSONHOOD

Yeah, you may say, but isn't this all very idealistic? Actually, no. What is idealistic is the image of the family and all the assumptions its members make. What is realistic is that when we are true to ourselves and understand why anything else doesn't make sense, we don't hurt forever. We can withstand setbacks, such as a separation or a divorce. We can feel alone but not lonely. We can be honest with a new friend.

When adults and their parents go in for counseling together, such as in an alcohol treatment center, it is not approached by therapists as true "family therapy." That is because realism must prevail and the family hierarchy must be treated as obsolete. This kind of counseling is called "conjoint adult therapy." Family therapy involves kids who are still doing their childing and parents who are still doing their parenting. They are still an active family, subject to the needs of the parents as well as the children.

Once we are divorced, where do we put our energies in terms of our families? Who do we spend our time with? Where do we put our focus?

We need to focus on the reality at hand. If we insist on trying to retain or resurrect any of our previous family relationships, we will delay the opportunity for a full life. At the same time, if we have children, we are handing down the old message of adult child imprisonment in the family of origin.

Loving While Claiming Our "Rights of Passage"

Does decathexis mean that we will stop loving, seeing, enjoying, or depending on one another? Absolutely not! After all, who else has more of an investment in the relationship than mothers and fathers and sons and daughters and sisters and brothers? But let that relationship be what it is, if it is: the kind of great adult friendships that grow with age, experience, and sharing as equals. Rather than only paying lip services to rites of passage, such as graduation and marriage, we need to actively assume the "rights of passage" and move on from our families of origin, taking with us our titles of son, daughter, mother, or father, but leaving the active roles of sonning, daughtering, mothering, or fathering behind.

FAMILY FRIENDSHIPS

When we are able to leave behind the active family roles of our childhood and move into family friendships, we continue to nourish those friendships. We can treat them as real friendships that don't thrive on assumption and duty. Without care and attention to these relationships, it is easy to fall back into the familiar -ing way of relating, creating discomfort, resentment, and disagreement. Being realistic, we need to be alert to the interactions and dynamics within our family friendships, which do not occur in our other close friendships.

COMPARISONS

What kinds of demands do you make of your best friends? Do you make the same demands that you, as parent or adult child, make of your children or your parents? Looking at that issue can be very enlightening.

Do we as parents or adult children treat one another as we would our closest and dearest friends? Let's ask some questions of ourselves regarding our friends and see if the behaviors toward our parents and our children are similar or identical. They should be, unless we have some very close friends we're parenting or being parented by!

In other words, try answering the following questions regarding your three closest friends—questions that deal with parenting, familying, and childing—and experience how unrealistic it is to attempt carrying out our roles with other family members into adulthood. The first set of questions are those dealing with parents, reflecting common expectations from their adult children.

Would you expect your best friend to:

- Interrupt each weekend for a visit with you?
- Borrow money and not repay it?
- Drive or fly 1,800 miles to see you every vacation, Thanksgiving, or Christmas?
- Need, want, and accept advice every time you feel compelled to give it to them?
- Accept your requirements for the relationship without question and stay in a support role most of the time?
- Strive and sacrifice to meet educational, occupational, materialistic, and social goals that you have set up for them?
- Follow in your footsteps and model after you?

Doesn't it sound slightly ridiculous in this perspective? Yet society says this ridiculous behavior is okay from parents, since childing creates a debt that can never be repaid with love alone; however, the only suitable sacrifice is the adult child's integrity. It's hard to feel qualified to stand on your own two feet when the foundation of your life is warped with this kind of conditioning.

Conversely, parents themselves may bear an unrealistic burden of expectations from their children when this continuity of role playing exists. The following questions might be used as a reality test by adult children who are still dependent on parents when gauging the appropriateness of their need.

Would you expect a friend to:

- Give you a loan on top of a loan?
- Babysit on the Friday of your choice?
- Have you to dinner every holiday?

- Give you his or her car whenever yours doesn't work?
- Let you drop in unannounced for lunch or dinner?
- Take your kids shopping for clothes at your request?
- Get one of your kids out of jail in the middle of the night?
- Let your kids walk on the furniture, play tag in their house, or slide on varnished floors?
- Keep their refrigerator stocked for your kids to raid?
- Let your kids rifle through bureau drawers and ask for what they fancy?
- Let you store your stuff in their garage year after year?
- Put their needs as a couple secondary to yours as an individual?

Another unlikely set of behaviors to be found among friends is that of always checking in on, checking up on, reporting in to, and reporting to one another (as both children or parents may feel is necessary). We're not talking about the fun closeness of best friends by anxious constant contact. Would a good friend who cares about me, respects my personal life and my independence cling or snoop like this? Would I do this to a friend?

Unconditional Love and Total Decathexis

The unconditional caring and love that occurs in friendships are rare among parents and their adult children. Individuation—becoming your own person—is a time for joy, for recognizing, feeling, and celebrating your own maturity and personhood. Decathexis—a reality-based separation for purposes of freedom—is a hallmark of having made it as a human being. If we learn to decathect and to celebrate ourselves as separate, unique individuals, we can love and be loved by family members without the need to cling to a family when its "operating" time is over. Knowing that we are whole and complete within ourselves, we can move with candor, serenity, and joy in and out of our various families.

Many societies celebrate decathexis and perform a separation ceremony within the family unit. A majority of parents and their children in most societies, however, have accepted the subjective "rightness" of ignoring this need or of minimizing its importance. Even though we have bas and bar mitzvahs, graduations, and weddings, we rarely let loose our old roles. Indeed, there is often the need for reassurance that everything will stay the same, as the tears flow. ("My little girl! I can't believe she's graduating from college!")

If family members have not gone through decathexis when they physically left home, it still isn't too late. You can decathect from your parents when you're twenty-eight, thirty-five, or fifty-seven. As a parent you can decathect from your adult children at any time. But late decathexis is a radical change from the enmeshed family pattern of expectations that has become a way of life. As a result, it can have its moments of pain and indecision.

Care and caution and full explanations to other family members may be necessary. Professional counseling would be useful in some very entangled families, and it is available if needed. The rewards of greater personal growth and self-esteem justify the effort and the investment.

The concept of unconditional love and total decathexis is well stated by Kahlil Gibran in *The Prophet*:

> Your children are not your children.
> They are the sons and daughters of
>   life's longing for itself.
> They come through you but not from you,
>   and though they are with you,
>   yet they belong not to you.

You may give them your love but not your thoughts,
    for they have their own thoughts.
You may house their bodies but not their souls,
    for their souls dwell in the House of Tomorrow,
    which you cannot visit,
    not even in your dreams.
You may strive to be like them,
    but seek not to make them like you.
For life goes not backward
    nor tarries with yesterday.
You are the bows from which your children
    as living arrows are sent forth.
The Archer sees the mark upon the path of the
    Infinite. And He bends you with His
    might that His arrows may go swift and far.
Let your bending in the Archer's hand
    be for gladness;
For even as He loves the arrow that flies,
    so He loves also the bow that is stable.[2]

COMMON FEELINGS

Following are some feelings that are remarkably common to both divorce trauma and family cathexis:

- *Hurt* is a catch-all expression, but generally it's the result of feeling a loss of respect.
- *Anxiety* is the fear of being hurt or of losing something essential to one's happiness. Whether it is reality based or not, it feels the same. It alerts us to defend ourselves.
- *Anger* is very often a response to being hurt. It is high-octane irritation and annoyance. Anger not resolved becomes rage.

• **Guilt** is the feeling of being unworthy or bad, or of being perceived as bad. It is repressed anger turned inward. It is being sorry about something you did or couldn't do. It is about a bad deed, while shame is feeling that you are the bad deed.

Actualizing the New You

Strength begins with self-ownership and pride that we act true to our feelings in our most important relationships. No one owns us, no matter what our relationship with them might be. We are not here on this planet to fulfill the unmet dreams of a parent or to protect another person from facing the reality of herself or himself in the world.

We do seem to be here to be ourselves and not someone else, to develop and grow, to be as honest and true to our real feelings as we possibly can dare. The tremendous diversity and uniqueness of individuals is the miracle of humanity—our built-in self-worth, just waiting to be appreciated. We crumble in crises like divorce only if we're talked into believing our worth is bestowed upon us by others. We can make the world a better place to live only if we first learn how to live our own lives freely.

What is it you want for yourself in this life? What are you doing to get it? What's in your way? Who put your stumbling blocks in place? Why have you waited for a crisis to force you to act?

These are tough questions, but the process of answering them leads to emotional self-sufficiency and new, loving relationships. Tossing out the deadwood of family misconceptions takes a strong arm. But by carting around the burdens that aren't rightly yours for so long, you may have built up just the muscle you need. Now is the time for a good emotional workout. As we clear away the practical and emotional complications of our divorces and our family independence issues, each of us is able to discover that "I am worthwhile simply because I am!"

15
CHOOSING TO LIVE SINGLE

*M*y mentor, Virginia Satir, once said, "I believe that divorce is not necessarily a failure, that it may also be a solution or a release." This statement is reminiscent in the results I have seen in the counseling work that I was honored to be part of for so many years. In many instances it became clear that a marriage was either built on a dysfunctional foundation or it became painful as two people grew in very different directions.

Dysfunctional Foundation

Throughout the course of my career, I have repeatedly met couples who've married because:

- It was expected by family, friends, and culture.
- They were expecting a baby.
- They didn't know how to live successfully on their own.
- They came from a painful family and wanted to get away.
- One or both of them wanted to have a child.

These are but a few among a number of other countless reasons.

The couples often explained that expectations and their early experiences with sex encouraged them to fall into their marriages, rather than assisting them in a lifestyle choice. Then, years later, they found themselves in an arrangement rather than a passionate, loving, and intimate connection with their partners. Ultimately, they chose to divorce.

> You have brains in your head. You have feet in your shoes.
> You can steer yourself in any direction you choose.
> You're on your own. And you know what you know.
> You are the one who will decide where to go.
>
> DR. SEUSS

Kim grew up in a family with an alcoholic father and a mother who was extremely passive. Her family looked like it was functional, as her father never lost his job or received a DWI citation of any kind. He paid all the family bills, and Kim's mother took care of the family and the home. Later in life, she worked as a substitute teacher. She took the fairly small paycheck she earned and spent it on special things for the children and occasionally for herself. Kim watched and learned. She was very intelligent and successful in high school and her first two years of college. During this time, she began making some subtle discoveries about herself.

She learned that she wanted to marry someone who did not drink and would provide for her. She met Todd, who was older and established in a good job. He didn't drink. Kim became obsessed with Todd and wanted to make sure he was the one for her. Even with all the birth control available to women today, she decided to have a baby without Todd's consent. When she became pregnant, Todd asked her to marry him. She dropped out of college, married, and became a mom.

The early years were good. Everything was new and she felt that Todd would always be there for her. Perhaps he would have been; however, after her two children started school and began to have schedules and activities of their own, Kim realized that Todd and her children had a purpose and were building lives beyond the home. She became unsatisfied and restless.

Todd had his work friends, belonged to the gym, and traveled for business. He had an interesting life. Both of their children were involved in sports, took dance classes, or were part of their own social groups. Even though Kim and Todd had friends, Kim felt empty. Ultimately, they began counseling and getting professional help. In a matter of months, they realized they really had never chosen the married life. They drifted into all of their decisions and, in truth, neither of them wanted to be married—to each other or to anyone else, for that matter. They both felt they had never had an opportunity to be single. They went straight from college to marriage and parenting. They both wanted out of the marriage.

Their situation was complicated because they had two wonderful children. Because of the love for their children, their counseling changed direction from marital counseling to divorce counseling, teaching them all the best possible ways to parent their children as two singles. Today they are both single and doing a wonderful job of parenting. In one counseling session, their children reported to me that they are much happier now that their parents were, too.

> Some people think it's holding on
> that makes one strong. Sometimes it's letting go.
> SYLVIA ROBINSON

New Faces of the Single Life

As I was doing research to better understand single life, I found new words that have been written to describe the state of being single. Some refer to it as "singlehood" or "singlism," and single people are sometimes called "singletons." Perhaps these will eventually be additions to our language and become part of our common usage. Whatever we call it, being single has quickly become a lifestyle that is growing in great numbers. In addition to the status of being single following a divorce, many are choosing this lifestyle for many reasons:

- They want to experience the single lifestyle.
- They want to concentrate on their education and careers without outside responsibilities.

- They want to be mobile, able to travel and relocate without commitment.
- They have retired, lost their mates, and want now to care only for themselves and do many things they haven't done before.
- They have been married and tied to the needs of others and now want the freedom to search for and find who they are as individuals.

> Choosing one path means giving up another.
>
> JEAN SHINODA-BOLEN

EXAMPLE 1:

Liz is twenty-nine years old. She worked herself through college and began the search for a job with her career desires in mind. She held a couple of jobs until she found one that was promising. She has been dating Kevin throughout her journey thus far. Shortly after starting her new career, Kevin has expressed his desire for them to marry and have two or three children while he pursues his career. Liz is conflicted and trying to work through all of her feelings. Her new job includes travel and opportunities to move up in the company. She has made the decision to postpone marriage and has shared her feelings with Kevin. He is very understanding and supportive of her choice.

Kevin and Liz have decided to both be free to date other people. Liz has moved into a one-bedroom apartment in Chicago's Lakeview neighborhood, where thousands of other singles live. She joined a book club, goes out to eat with girlfriends, and has a regular fitness program. She says it's not that she will never marry, but right now she wants to be single, enjoy herself, experiment with life, and learn to financially take care of herself.

For young men and women never married, having a place of one's own is a mark of adulthood and success. Knowing you can care for yourself financially is a part of developing self-worth and making a healthy transition to adulthood. Marriage between equals at a later stage in life just might provide a better chance of satisfaction and happiness than falling into an early marriage.

> Balancing your life between work, play, spirituality, exercise, and relationships helps you to grow and feel joy.
>
> DOREEN VIRTUE

EXAMPLE 2:

Judy lives in a fifty-five-plus neighborhood. She was only fifty when she moved in, but her husband was older and was the qualifying partner. Dan and Judy loved their life together in this community. They met many other couples with similar interests, activities, and zest for life. Judy's children lived out of state, so their community became their second family.

When Dan died only five years later, Judy was devastated. Not only did she lose Dan (who was her best friend), she also lost her role as half of a couple that socialized, played, traveled, and supported each other.

While working out at the gym about a year after Dan's death, one of the women who lived in the community was on the machine next to her and asked if she was doing any dating. Judy replied that she had not and wasn't even all that interested; however, her friend persisted and invited both Judy and her friend Brian for dinner a couple of weeks later. They both accepted and found that they really hit it off.

Over the next few months, Judy and Brian saw many movies, enjoyed dinner together, found TV shows they enjoyed watching together, and they even went on one cruise together; however, even though they enjoyed each other's company and support, neither of them wanted to marry. Judy's memories of her husband were too great and Brian really loved his single life. He taught part-time classes, traveled often to see his children, and had been single for many years following the early death of his wife. Both Brian and Judy had gotten quite used to and enjoyed the single life. Their years of commitment to a spouse were over.

Judy and Brian are an example of many older relationships that have developed over the last twenty or thirty years. They care for each other, they support each other (in sickness and in health), they have fun together, and they bring each other a great deal of companionship. Still, they choose to be single at this stage in their lives.

A Changing Culture

Statistics, as reported in the January 2012 edition of *Fortune* magazine, tell us that we are becoming an increasingly solo nation. Americans are now within mere percentage points of being a majority single nation: Only 51 percent of adults today are married, according to census data. And 28 percent of all households now consist of just one person—the highest level in U.S. history. The extraordinary rise of living alone is among the greatest of social changes since the baby boom.

Living solo is now shaping our families and our communities. The single person is often more likely to eat out, buy a gym membership, take new classes, and support cultural endeavors. With more disposable income, time, and a variety of interests, they bring both creativity and spending to the table. Even culture is adding recognition to the single woman. DeBeers, which has always provided diamonds as the embodiment of a couple's romantic bond, has now offered a "right-hand ring" for unmarried women who want to treat themselves to elegant jewelry.

Single life is living alone, but not being lonely. It is more of a collective experience. In many cities, retirement communities, and even in Middle America, there are what is known as "tribes." In my earlier writings, I referred to these groups of people as "families of choice." Some are female tribes, some are male tribes, and many are mixed genders. These are people who have come together through common interests (books, sports, wine tasting, volunteer work, travel clubs, movie critics, etc.). They develop as social networks and fulfill many needs for their members. With many families being at a distance with their siblings and blood relatives, these tribes become like a family unit. Sometimes a couple is in the group, but many of the members are most likely single.

Also in our frequent 24/7 work culture is a fine line between who are personal and who are professional friends. So often the most frequent and meaningful relationships are coworkers, while home is used for sleep, quiet time, and regrouping. This style fits well for the single person. Loneliness is not an issue. One middle-aged woman shared with me that there is nothing lonelier than living in the wrong relationship. Another woman said to me, "I like having a man in my life, just not in my home. . . . I would rather be alone and happy in my life than miserable in a relationship."

> Life may not be the party we hoped for,
> but while we are here, we should dance.
>
> UNKNOWN

Currently several websites and magazines address the joy and celebration of living a single life. While many people choose it early in life, it seems to be a very good path for a newly divorced person to walk. The journey to knowing how to live single and be successful in every way doing so is probably the best training, should one choose to marry again. Being single is a skill and an art. It is also a valued lifestyle.

Tips for the Divorced Person

If you are newly divorced, here are a few tips:

- Give up language or thoughts of losing your "other half." You are whole yourself. Find that part of yourself that had merged with another and bring it back to life.
- Find someone to do all the tasks in your home and with your car that you can't do yourself. Call them handymen, cooks, housekeepers, etc. Don't plan to do everything by yourself.
- Join AAA, take cooking classes, or have meals delivered, and sign up for gym classes just because it feels good.
- Take down old photos that have anything to do with the past and replace them with current shots of yourself as you develop your new life. Add new music to your iPod, and get rid of any music that reminds you of your old life.
- Get an emergency contact and plan for anything you might need. Friends, neighbors, and tribes are good places to start. Ask for help and be willing to give it.
- Recognize that you may be single, but you are never alone. Write down your list that includes your "family of choice" and say a grateful prayer each day.

16
DATING, SEXUALITY, AND REMARRIAGE

Joan: There were just too many problems unresolved from both my family and my first marriage, so my second marriage also fell apart. He was a nice man, but the bulk of the finances was on my shoulders. After counseling we still got divorced because then we could clearly see that we just didn't mesh. I was single for a few years after this second divorce, but it wasn't the painful experience I had after my first marriage. I began seeing myself as a survivor instead of a bad person and a failure. I felt like a personal success story just to be raising my children to healthy adulthood.

After I became established professionally and knew what I could achieve, I felt like a complete person. I was actually enjoying the single life. My time alone was really very important as I was becoming more mature. Just when I figured I'd probably be alone for the rest of my life—and could enjoy that—along came my soul mate! I was now ready for him. I could take as well as give, and give freely, without feeling anything I did would be inadequate.

When we married, it was like for the first time. My other two marriages had to do with fulfilling painful needs. This one was about two independent people who understood themselves coming together. Yes, we had to negotiate and make compromises. But we were able to do that. We were both strong and we had both healed from our pasts.

Ken: I cannot believe I have made as many choices, decisions, and changes as I have in the last twelve years. It's a separate life, in many ways. I know I could live happily today being single, but after some time I found a woman I just had to ask to marry me. We had a lot of difficulty in our early years together from my children's resistance to her. They didn't want me marrying anyone in general, and her especially.

For a long time I felt pulled between my children, who wanted me to return to their mother, and the woman who loved me. I was still in therapy when I remarried, and it finally sank in that I had to be true to myself or no one would ultimately be satisfied.

Kathy: I was so much more ready for sharing my life with someone when I met my second husband. Sharing children with two families is nothing I could have handled before. I wasn't even conscious of what intimacy, relationship, or responsibility were at the time I married Jim.

Doyle and I now have a beautiful little child of our own, Tommy, who is the full-time resident. This causes some problems with my two stepchildren. I have to reassure them that Tommy is not any closer to us than they are, just because he was born to both of us. I try to make the stepchildren feel equally loved and I treat them all the same way. I took a chance with this marriage under these circumstances, and I give myself a lot of credit for being able to make it work.

Bob: After my first marriage flopped, I dated a lot. A real lot. I was almost afraid of remarriage. There was no way I wanted to go through the pain and bitterness again. But after a while I thought less and less about what had happened in terms of how it still affected me. I was very cautious about getting serious with a woman again, but I was also feeling more confident about myself. I was not the person who made that first mistake. By the time I decided to marry Suzie, I had really done some soul-searching and had discarded a lot of deadwood out of my system.

I can truthfully say I have never felt as much trust and fulfillment with someone as I have in my marriage today. Occasionally we have a flare-up, but we don't worry about those. We're still two different people. I have a solid relationship with my wife, and I intend to honor that at all costs.

Suzie has two kids and we have one together. Everyone understands this is a team effort. We never let the kids come between us. We know they will grow up and leave, and we will still be here together. My wife's a full partner with me in all the decisions we make about the kids or otherwise. We are enjoying life.

The Prospects of Dating Again

One of the scariest features of divorce for many ex-spouses can be the prospect of dating again. We sense that something is different out there. We know we are different. It's been a while since we were totally footloose with no emotional ties, no promises, or exclusive arrangements. Suddenly we are part of a singles scene, which, by the way, seems to include a lot of people younger than we are.

TAKE IT EASY AT FIRST

If this were a perfect world where no temptations crossed our paths until we were ready to deal with them, we could wait a year before seriously dating anyone. That's what 83 percent of the ex-spouses I surveyed recommended. They pointed out that several personal concerns really should be ironed out before we're in the best position to tackle a relationship that could get serious. Some good reasons they felt ex-spouses should take it easy with dating in the first year include the probabilities that:

- We're still on an emotional roller coaster.
- We're confused.
- We have a need for self-care.
- Multiple changes in our lives are taking up our attention.
- We may be trying to reorder our priorities in life.
- Our family healing needs attention.

- Our financial changes may make a difference.
- Our work concerns may be all the extra pressure we can handle.

Relationships—even lighthearted ones—take time and energy. Most of the participants in my survey recommended socializing in groups, attending parties and dinners, but not yet getting emotionally involved with one person.

An interest in making new friends and an interest in dating are, of course, not the same. The person who is only looking for new friends is focused on socializing. The person who is looking for a mate is dating and needs to be prepared for the difference. Looking for friendships is a pleasure and socializing is fun. If you are focused on finding a new partner, add the elements of excitement but also concern. Then you may feel some pressure to be and look your best and to evaluate more critically the person you are with.

Do you need the extra complications of dating right now, as welcome and ego-boosting a distraction as it may be? If you just want to socialize, you can ask people over. If you're angling for a serious relationship, then you may feel it necessary to take the traditional stance of waiting to be asked out. This imposes its own limits and probably adds frustrations to your efforts to build a new circle of friends. Learning to enjoy your own company and casual socializing first helps build a stronger foundation for a possible future partnership.

> *Premature dating after divorce can lead to regrets that you weren't fully ready for a new relationship. Casual socializing gives you more time to get used to yourself as single.*

As the months go by and healing takes place, you will feel the confidence rising in your new identity. This is the ideal time to enjoy your single status and take on the "responsibility" of dating relationships or another coupleship.

WAYS TO MEET A NEW PARTNER

They are endless, but in case you've forgotten:

1. Wear or carry a conversation piece—a book, an unusual umbrella, a piece of jewelry, a small dog (doubles as protection!).
2. Find out what makes you feel more desirable. Whether it's a neat pair of lucky suspenders, a silk shirt, or lingerie by Victoria's Secret, when you feel desirable, you will come across as more desirable.
3. Tell your friends that you are dating.
4. Take a singles' vacation. There are all kinds of singles' trips that are often put together around particular activities, such as deep-sea fishing, camping, photography, or hiking. You might not only meet someone but you'll have a good time while you are doing it.

Coupleship and Remarriage in the Twenty-First Century

Chances are you will find that relationships today are quite different compared with those of the 1990s, '80s, or '70s, not to mention the '60s. Back in the '60s and through much of the '70s, the sexual revolution was in full swing. Sex had a very high priority in relationships.

By the '80s, many couples were running out of steam. Lack of desire rapidly became the number one sexual complaint, and it continued to be a concern in the '90s. The economy, high personal debt levels, and job burnout are part of the problem as layoffs and cutbacks force more work into the hands of fewer people. Also, many people in the '80s had a more specific commitment to their jobs—and to their fitness clubs—than they had to one another. After scrambling to get too much done at work, couples then tried to wedge intimacy, closeness, emotional fulfillment, and sex, maybe, into the half-hour between 11 and 11:30 at night. There is also concern and necessary fear surrounding AIDS.

Maybe the good news about couples' downshifting from the sexual revolution is that people are beginning to find there's more to partnering, more to relationships, and more to life than sex-in-overdrive. Sometimes sexual enjoyment is still a high-priority item, but there's more tolerance now for an ebb and flow that acknowledges additional commitments of our energies. Just because other interests are taking priority doesn't mean that love is out the window.

Couples aren't necessarily suffering from dysfunctional sexual lives, but may be suffering from dysfunctional lifestyles.

As you begin dating, you may well find that sexual norms have changed from your pre-marriage days. Rather than finding people who know all there is to know about the mechanics of sex, you may encounter more who are looking for a relationship that emphasizes the whole person. They don't want to work so hard at being sexual. Relaxation, conversation, touch, hugs—more of a whole body experience with each other is popular. With this comes more complete intimacy—a surprise to many who felt they had to work for it—and more sexual satisfaction. Sex today tends to go beyond the climax-oriented sex of the '60s and '70s to a physical relationship that bonds body, mind, heart, and spirit.

TUNING IN

Despite all that's been written in magazines, newspapers, and books about being close and being sexual, I've found many couples continuing to enter a relationship or partnership without the foggiest notion of what togetherness is all about. In my book *Intimacy and Sexuality*,[1] I give information about the understanding of couples that I obtained during my years as a marriage and family therapist. If you want to get back on track with touch as a means of communication, you might want to review some of the areas that bogged you down and were not working in your marriage.

Communicating at various levels is often a problem. When couples with marriage difficulties come to me and say, "We have problems with communication," it almost always translates to, "We can't talk about our sexual relationship. We talk around it, as we do around our other kinds of blocks."

The first step in solving a communications problem with someone else is to solve it with yourself. Many of us can't even communicate our needs to ourselves. We may hide from one feeling to gratify another. But if you can't have an honest relationship with yourself, it's even harder to have one with someone else. By pulling out all the feelings, including the contradictory ones, and sharing them with yourself and then others, a full picture of a real loveable person will emerge.

We have many, many feelings every single day, yet most of us talk about only a few: mad, sad, guilty, hurt, and ashamed. All the rest are actually the language of intimacy, the ones that explain the others. Be fully aware of how you think, what you feel, and how you behave, then work on the ability to share that with another.

PASS THE PASSION

The capacity to share our feelings is the basis of the word passion. Check out its meaning in the dictionary and you may be surprised.

You can increase your passion potential by taking the time to feel aspects of life you might have been missing. I know that I've experienced passion at seeing beautiful sunsets, experiencing natural childbirth, being a part of the birth of my grandchildren, and by listening to some fantastic music. That, to me, brings about thoroughly passionate feelings on a par with sexual enjoyment. Narrowing our passionate expectations to just one area of expressions stunts us. When listening

Passion means "full of feeling" not just lust or excitement. Being passionate is being yourself, freed of the emotion-blocking burdens of the past.

to great music, not only can we hear it, but we expand our sensory appreciation to feel it with our entire bodies as well. Opening ourselves to a fuller range of feelings helps us open up the others and experience them on a deeper level.

When we feel our feelings, not just observe them, we release ourselves to more passion. This means we have to admit the painful feelings, too—agony, despair, and loss—acknowledging both ends of the spectrum from ecstasy to despair. We can't improve our passion potential by editing out the feelings we'd rather not have. Passion is about fullness, not about holding back.

To develop the capacity to enjoy a rich relationship with someone special, we can exercise our feelings by having a full-body experience with people we meet. When you are close to someone, practice your awareness of what they project. Our energy fields extend about three feet around us and can send messages as clear as "I'm angry," "I'm at ease," and even "I'm not tuned into anything!"

Blending is the process that happens when we feel our own passion and another's, when we are able to express our feelings and find that they tune in to the same frequency as our partners. You can trust blending as a safe experience when you can trust yourself to feel more fully.

TRUST AND SAFETY FIRST

Healthy people don't just walk up and expose their deeper feelings to any willing listener. Correspondingly, emotionally sound people don't do this with their bodies, either. Most of the time, after feelings of safety and trust have been proven sound, some kind of commitment develops: to care for each other, to be honest with each other, and to nourish each other. As we become closer, this commitment increases the flow of passion.

EMOTIONAL INTERCOURSE AND TRUST

A bonding of feelings is what everybody seems to want, but it just doesn't happen with physical or mechanical intercourse. People can have a lot of sexual activity and yet say, "I still feel so empty! I still feel so lonely!" Their hunger is a lack of intimacy, an unfulfilled need to be vulnerable with another person and to know that they're safe in this relationship of trust. In a commitment to care about each other, two people are able to use their sensory systems to move from sharing and intimacy to emotional intercourse. Then a truly full physical intercourse occurs that mirrors the mutually satisfying emotional sharing that is underway.

Sometimes the recently divorced, who are still caught up in feelings of betrayal, have trouble trusting a new lover. As a result, sexual enjoyment may be fleeting. When the betrayal issue is worked out, we learn to trust ourselves again because of the understanding we've gained. We stop attaching negative expectations to members of the

opposite sex just because of our former spouses' behaviors. When we
understand what went wrong with
our previous marriages, we put ourselves in a position to trust ourselves
and others.

> *When two people are able to share their feelings in an atmosphere of safety and trust, they are enjoying real intimacy or emotional intercourse.*

FOCUSING ON OUR SEXUALITY

Trust is necessary to maximize our use of sensate focus. If we are
worrying about our new partner also betraying us, we cannot focus
on sexual enjoyment. Our sensory system is sidetracked. When our
sensory system is fully attuned, this faculty available to us is called
sensate focus. It enables us to concentrate on any part of ourselves
and make it work for us. If you want to focus on a sight, a sound, or
a smell, you can with this power.

When we are interested in achieving sexual enjoyment, we direct
sensate focus to the genitals. If we are feeling safety, trust, and commitment, and we are feeling very good about the intimacy that we
have with someone else, we have the ability to sensate focus on our
genitals and become physically aroused consistently, not just the first
few times.

When we are aware of both of these two elements necessary
for continued sexual enjoyment, we see that we, ourselves, play an
important part in our own pleasuring.

We ourselves have to bring sensate focus to the relationship and
have as a partner someone with whom we feel so safe that this focus
is easy. Every female, therefore, has the responsibility to bring about
the conditions for her own arousal. Every male has the responsibility
to bring about the conditions for his own arousal.

It is not just the other person's responsibility to arouse us. Our minds and hearts must be centered on our capacity to respond.

When each person has taken the responsibility for her or his own arousal system, there is an emotional and physical consequence, otherwise known as an orgasm, a full-body orgasm. This is not just a mechanical high, since it can be felt in the fingertips, in the toes, in the entire body, as well as the genitals. With that often comes an emotional high, which is equally satisfying and pleasurable.

Often in relationships that aren't quite right, an orgasm is followed by an abrupt sense of separation. Although we'd burn out if a climax didn't end sometime, partners in a relationship of trust and love return to where they started from after an orgasm, into an atmosphere of intimacy and a feeling of safety, trust, and commitment. And when this happens, they are then able to move into what I call emotional afterplay.

EMOTIONAL AFTERPLAY

The first twenty or thirty minutes following intercourse that results in climax is a highly sensitized time. We are sensitized physically and emotionally. It is a time that can be best used to create further bonding and trust for the couple. This can be done by:

- Sharing more with each other
- Telling each other something very personal
- Letting the other know of the love you feel

What a wonderful bonding time—there's none better! Let's tell our partners how much we care about them and what they mean to us. Affirm the person's specialness. A speech isn't necessary, just a few heartfelt words. As a relationship progresses and people get more and more comfortable with this kind of sharing after intercourse, they can make it a fun time. They can be silly with each other. They can play with the other's child within. They can laugh and have a good time, just like two little children who are able to enjoy each other without pretense or rules.

Each experience of trust and joy, along with the bonding of affirmation, cements commitment and nourishes love. It helps people retain and build on their ability to be passionate. It is a wonderful truism that the longer a couple has intercourse in real intimacy, affirming of each other's worth, the more passionate they become. The older they get and the longer they are in a committed relationship, the more their fullness of feeling stays full.

Sexual Relationships That Aren't Safe

It's hardly unusual to find people having sexual relationships with partners they barely know, much less trust. Seductions, affairs, and short-term contacts are common not only because people are interested in becoming close to someone but also because these relationships are new, exciting, possibly secretive, and they make us feel intensely, even if briefly. They are an easy fix with no personal investment necessary. They require no previous commitment to ourselves, no self-understanding, no "other" understanding; however, many people find that as soon as familiarity sets in— guess what? The connection doesn't

Passion based on caring and trust doesn't diminish with age or time. The opposite happens: each passionate experience is a coin that adds to our sexual wealth.

excite anymore. It's all external, nothing to do with anything real and lasting.

The unworkability of these relationships may be smothered in impossibly idealistic fantasies of romance: "She is exquisitely sensitive!" or emotional stimulation due to dangerous circumstances: "Her husband sits behind me at work!" or their novelty: "He's a race driver!" or sheer physical attractiveness: "He is six foot two and looks like a Greek god!" Sometimes the fact that the person is totally unknown is the prime stimulation: "I just met this person and she really turns me on!"

THE TRAP OF NOVELTY ROMANCES

All these novelty feelings may make those whose lives are sluggish feel vibrantly alive so that their sensate focus can be activated. But the focus remains only as long as the emotional newness of it survives. This syndrome is frustrating and filled with shame as we move on from person to person to person in order to feel something.

People may seek short-term relationships for a number of reasons. Their past may include emotional trauma in which trust has been broken, commitment has been betrayed, and closeness brought hurt and emotional pain. Closeness no longer feels safe.

SHUTDOWNS

We can also be shut down because of sexual abuse or emotion "medicators," like alcohol, drugs, and nicotine. Nicotine and cocaine are very powerful repressors of emotions. Workaholism and food disorders also repress feelings. There are many medicators, some behavioral and some chemical. All of them work in the same way, making our feelings unavailable to us. Even constant busyness, frenetic activity, excessive exercising, and bodybuilding can put a cap on the feelings that contribute to intimacy.

MECHANICAL SEX

Mechanical sex is sex that takes place outside of a person's emotional range. The stimulus for arousal comes from our minds, even though a sense of lack may prompt the need. If we have shut down as a result from physical or emotional medicators, we have to rely on artificial stimulation to become aroused. The most frequent artificial stimulations are chronic masturbation, pornography, affairs, seductions, violence, and danger (e.g., living on the edge).

The partner of someone involved in mechanical stimulation naturally finds sex much less satisfying. One reason is that it is the norm for men to be stimulated faster, most of the time, than females. When one person reaches climax before the other (who may feel either angry, hurt, or left out), there is no way for them to become really fulfilled. Certainly not emotionally. Even sex between two people without emotional intercourse is not much more than masturbation. Climax becomes a mere product, a physical release, period!

Then comes a letdown. When there was no intimacy to begin with, the letdown is often painful. The relationship may have started out as two people with parallel desires to somehow connect, but they were never able to share their feelings and build anything more than a limited intimacy. Their sexual coupling is dependent on artificial stimulation. After climax, their feelings head downhill. Both people may begin to feel a certain sense of discomfort. Here you are in a very close, intimate place with another person, and you have no idea how that person is really feeling about you. There was no talk about feelings (other than sexual) before, and there's none now. It's a place that doesn't feel good, except if you have determined it's better than having to face your problems with intimacy.

VIOLENT "LOVERS"

Another kind of dysfunctional relationship is both exciting and dangerous enough to stimulate emotional bonding for some people. The arguing couple who suddenly become "lovebirds" is often symptomatic of people who need a powerful fight to arouse their sense of connectedness. Only when the other has screamed loudly enough to show "caring" can their sensate focus really kick in. Perhaps they had parents who set this pattern as "normal" and weren't able to create much self-esteem in their youngsters. Unfortunately, a relationship like this can go on indefinitely. But who would want it to?

Figure 16.1. Medicators

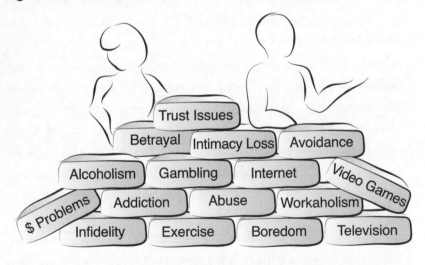

SEXUAL ATROPHY: A PATTERN FROM THE PAST?

A recent study showed that the single most common sexual problem reported to marriage counselors by couples in the United States was a lack of desire. "Too busy" or "not interested" were frequent responses. After a while, people adjust to almost anything, including something so basic as sex or lack of it. They develop a sort of comfortable arrangement in which there is silent agreement not to even talk about it anymore. Then one partner notices that two months have passed since any intimacy. Three months have gone by. Six months have gone by. A year has passed since there has been any kind of passionate connection. The reason behind the indifference may be so painful that eventually closeness is avoided altogether.

Divorced partners may have built up a negative response to sexual contact based on a long time of avoiding a problem partner. If this is you, give yourself a chance to break the momentum of avoidance or apathy. Negative habits can take a while to deprogram from our system, just as they took some time to become established.

SEXUAL RECOVERY

One person cannot have a meaningful relationship for two. Both people need to make whatever commitment for trust and safety is necessary for them to broaden their understanding and enjoyment of each other.

If your sensory system is flagging, if you want to enjoy a close relationship with someone again, you'll need to revive and refresh your mind and body. Don't project your ex-partner's faults onto every new person you meet; some innocent comment may trigger memories that make us too self-protective. And drop your medicators. Each one of us has a medicator that helps us forget our emotional hot spots. If you hunger for a healthy relationship with someone, make that someone yourself first. Then you will have maximized your chances for success in the next partnership.

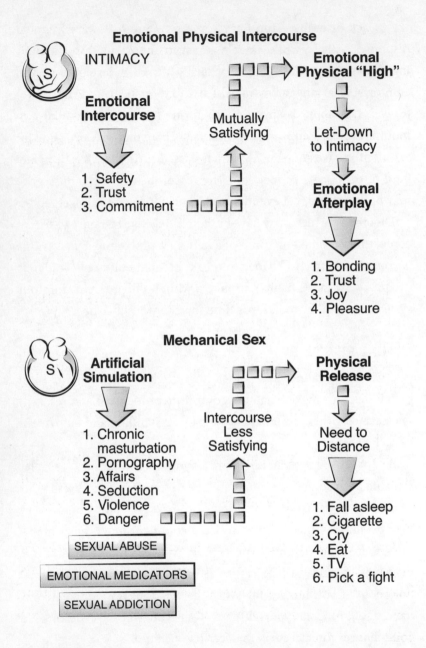

Figure 16.2. Sex

I have many concerns and much sadness for the people who look for intimacy while they are still smoking, drinking, overworking, or exercising to excess. It is impossible to reach intimacy while we are medicated. So, first, all medicators have to go! This is a reality test. Are you truly interested in intimacy? Or do you want a new kind of person in your life while holding on to the same mentality that attracted and maintained the old relationship? The choice may be easy, but doing it may take real desire.

Second, we have to find ways to express our feelings more deeply and more often. Newness can encourage us in this activity. Try new things; see new or old things in a new light; visit new places.

Analyze a painful feeling and see where it leads. Both painful and joyful feelings open us to new awareness and understanding. That's what forms us into the kind of people who have something to contribute to intimacy.

Feelings are frightening for a person who hasn't had them for a while or who has tried not to have them. Giving up our medicators lets our feelings surface. Try enjoying them in the emotional intimacy of physical closeness without intercourse. It is not necessary to have sex every single time we become physically affectionate, close, or emotional with each other. An understanding partner will let us become comfortable with this physical/emotional closeness without sex.

After we have achieved progress in our own personal recovery, then we can begin to look at what it means to achieve recovery in a relationship. That takes some renegotiation. "How much of my time am I going to spend on me personally, and how much time am I going to spend getting used to closeness?"

Figure 16.3. Prescription Medicators

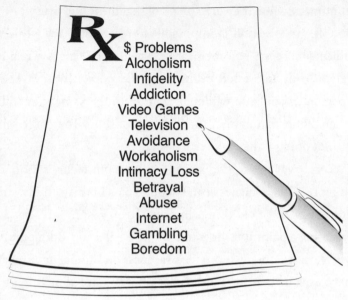

Relationships are a choice. Intimacy is a choice. Both are choices we can make, but then we need to commit time, energy, willingness, and integrity to that process.

How Much Time Does Intimacy Take?

Finding the right kind of sexual experience isn't like finding a pretty stone on the beach. People actually have to carve out time to create it. Those who do are the people who rate their relationships very high on their lists of important things in life. Many of the people who have achieved a highly satisfying sex life report that they spend at least 75 percent of their nonworking hours with their mates.

Many of us have been conditioned to feel that the more we do, the more we are. This philosophy won't help our relationships at all.

We have only one taskmaster. That is us. We're the ones who make commitments that reduce our personal time to a half-hour at night. Some people need to fit their commitment to their partners in with their exercise, housework, classes, or hobbies. After a divorce takes place, people want to make sure that they have quality time with their children. Add all of that up and pretty soon there is no time for partnering. That brings us to the issue, "Do I want a close relationship or don't I?"

If it's "I do," then it will take some time to devote to a second marriage or serious long-term relationship. When you do that, you may have to let some other activities go. Maybe the house will be a mess once in a while. Maybe the class won't be attended with as great a commitment. Maybe the fitness club will be visited twice a week, instead of five times a week.

Many people are coming to realize that we can't have it all, and in the twenty-first century, relationships need extra-sensitive treatment. If the relationship is going to work, and if it's going to be good, it will have to be a priority, which takes commitment and energy.

For a long time in marriage and intimacy counseling, there was the saying, "Before you can love anyone else, you have to be able to love yourself." That statement is still true, but now we hear another saying, "You will only be complete as you learn to love another." You cannot be completed by another, but when you acquire the capacity to be close, you will feel more fulfilled. Fear of intimacy and commitment is being recognized as a real impediment to personal growth.

We're not saying everybody has to go out and have a second relationship. Not everybody wants to do that. But for many people, having a clear, close, satisfying relationship is a very important ingredient in their emotional and physical health. Does this mean that if you decide to stay single you are destined to stay or become psychologically troubled? Of course not!

Happy Singlehood

Enjoying living alone is also an important trend, and there are many, many ways besides marriage to learn to love someone or to learn to connect meaningfully with others. We can learn to be very discriminating in our closest relationships and make sure that the intimate friendships we choose, regardless of the sex involved, are between strong, mutually respecting equals.

Many people, once they have been single, begin to grow in their own right. They thrive on the enjoyment of good friends, a rich life, and being in charge of themselves and their own time. One disadvantage is that other people often can't leave them alone and ask, "How come you're not married?" The following are several reasons you can give to vary "I don't want to be!":

1. I haven't been asked.
2. I won't settle for less.
3. I don't have the right dress.
4. Just lucky, I guess.
5. I still haven't given up a shot at the Miss America title.
6. I earn enough frequent flyer tickets only for one.
7. I'd have to forfeit my trust fund.
8. I'm married to my career.
9. I haven't your nerve.

Whether we want to stay single or not, singlehood is far superior to staying in a painful marriage. Singlehood gives us the room to grow unfettered in peace with no limits to our potential for self-created happiness. Divorce in this country is a stigma in very few places. Americans are famous for their practicality. If something doesn't work, fix it. If it can't be fixed, find something that does work. No intelligent person imagines divorce is the easy way out of a painful relationship, but it is often the only way to give our personhood and our sexuality the chance for healthy expression.

Choosing Remarriage

Aside from any children you might have, the greatest gift your ex-spouse might have given you (unintentionally!) is a firm sense of what you don't want in your next marriage. We all pretty much know the qualities we'd like to find, but there's nothing like a divorce to make it crystal clear what changes we want in our relationships.

So perhaps you would like to remarry. Undoubtedly, you're especially interested in not making a mistake. The presence of certain qualities in a person can reassure you that this time you are on the right track. The candidate who seems to be the most respectful of your differences—not just your similarities—in each other is most likely not to disappoint. This would also be someone who:

- Would say "I love you" spontaneously
- Would be patient with you as you try to make it in a new marriage
- Knows what he or she wants out of life, is willing to work for it, and is also willing to let you do the same, in your own way
- Is affectionate
- Doesn't want to change you and accepts you the way you are
- Will work with you in resolving issues around his children, her children, our children, or no children

Loving Relationships

Love is a friendship that has caught fire. It is quiet understanding, mutual confidence, sharing and forgiving. It is loyalty through the good times and bad. It settles for less than perfection and makes allowances for weaknesses. Love is content with the present, it hopes for the future, and doesn't brood over the past. If you have love in your life, it can make up for a great many things you lack. If you don't have it, no matter what else there is, it is not enough.

ANN LANDERS

HAPPY REMARRIAGE "SECRETS"

Frequently, couples who have been married a zillion years are asked, "What is your secret?" The happy pair may have narrowed their response down to something like "We never go to bed angry!" but it really takes a lot of "secrets" to make a marriage a success.

Someone has said, "Happiness is spending more time building relationships than worrying about losing them." With that in mind, here are ten "secrets" for a happy remarriage:

1. You know you are probably on your way to a healthy relationship if you immediately feel some sense of "being at home" with each other. Elementary to a lasting relationship is some sense of rapport, comfortableness, and ease.

2. A couple must share honor and respect for each other. Even when you think your mate is wrong or completely off base, you don't lose faith that at his or her core is honesty, fairness, and commitment. Long-lasting lovers always give each other the benefit of the doubt. If both of you feel that way, you probably have a solid foundation for your life together.

3. If the other's happiness is a high priority, if you desire with all your might that your partner succeed, do well at work, live and play in health, that's a good sign. Something about your partner has touched you profoundly. Wanting happiness and health for your mate, from the bottom of your heart, is a sign that you already love your partner.

4. Couples who are going to make it probably have lots of similarities and lots of differences. Their similarities provide a sense of comfort and ease, a tranquil ability to live with each other, day in and day out, through the ups and downs, and joys and traumas of life. Their differences provide excitement and challenge. Their different hobbies, different friends, and different outlooks on life enrich the relationship.

5. Couples really wanting to make marriage work face their problems and don't carry resentments. Each day is too short to stay angry, to indulge in the "silent treatment," or to nurse resentments. Breakfast is a great togetherness time of sharing coffee, maybe reading some meditation books, and then separating for the day. But, oh, what an exciting day when you know that in the evening, you each have a haven to return to—a little time together, a little candlelight, and being able to share the day's adventures with someone who cares. There is a sense of comfort that neither partner wants to muddy with grudges. When you know that what you have together is more than what you have with anyone else, you are well on your way to a long and happy relationship.

6. You aren't afraid of having routines. Some people think routines are boring and others think they are a part of inner peace. If you enjoy sharing routines or find more inner peace with your partner, you've probably found the right mate. Routines, in many ways, suggest trust and confidence. Although routines are shortcuts to happiness, they don't produce it, but they do enhance the ability

to trust your partner. They also become a very necessary
part of a healthy relationship.

7. There is some kind of a life dream. Life dreams can be very
short, like "Let's save everything we've got and take a trip
to Europe next fall!" or, "Let's save for three years and buy
ourselves that house in the country we always wanted to
have," or, "Maybe if we both work hard for a year or two we
will have the kind of stability that we'd like to have. Maybe
we wouldn't have to work so hard." Your dreams could be
wanting to work in such a way that you could retire at an
early age. Or maybe write a book or start a business together.
It really doesn't matter much what the dream is. What counts
is a common underlying desire and excitement about life.
Maybe there's even something the two of you could do
together that one probably wouldn't attempt alone.

People who share dreams tend to enjoy remarkably
happy marriages, much happier than most. Whatever the
content of the dream, it's the sharing and joint effort toward
it that make a couple feel a lot of fulfillment.

8. A major indicator of a happy couple is that they learn to roll
with the punches. Nobody has an easy, well-laid-out life that
just unfolds without any kind of trauma or stress. All kinds
of things come up. Many things can occur that work against
the relationship, too, such as problems with a job, finances,
adult children, or in-laws. Many stresses are also on a
marriage. Partners must decide very early, "Do we want a
coupleship or don't we?" If they do, they must "roll with the
punches" as they work out the coupleship.

It is very important for a couple to have certain principles
they will both stand by. Basically, they must protect the
marriage against all outside invasion. Many marriages
have been torn apart by outside influences, such as painful
relationships with children, "ex-anythings," job stress,

and financial difficulties. The couple needs to decide how important the relationship is, and if it is important, both partners' actions will support its survival.

9. The importance of sex and romance is not underestimated. Usually sex and romance have been what brought the couple together in the first place. It's the glue that keeps the partners focused on the coupleship. A good partnership rests upon the cherished qualities of daily intimacy: touching, hugs, comments like "I love you," and daily respect. Many couples will need to learn how vital it is to sneak away to movies, take long weekend vacations, or possibly go on ones that are very far away, buy little gifts or cards for each other, light candles, share in kitchen chores, or plan surprises for each other. There are so many things couples can do to enhance their relationship. You might take a look at my book Coupleship[2] for ideas on how to enhance romance within a marriage. If you scratch underneath the surface of a happy marriage, you will find a real chemistry and commitment to making it an exciting partnership.

The miracle of a coupleship full of meaning is that even though these people have an exclusive relationship and see each other day after day, boredom doesn't set in. Instead, the more that is added to romance and sex, the stronger the foundation of the partnership becomes. As life moves on and we move with it, our attraction to each other becomes greater, not lesser. There seems to be an interacting chemistry, a strong force that bonds people together throughout the years.

10. Couples who really make it in a relationship that fulfills both their needs do believe in and practice monogamy. In all my work with families and couples, plus the surveys that I have done, monogamy is one of the most important factors in a coupleship. Being faithful is not just something one chooses

to do. Being faithful, for happy couples, is the foundation upon which the marriage was built. It was a basic requirement.

When I began interviewing people on the subject of happy marriages, I had planned to accumulate quite a large variety of opinions on fidelity, its pros and cons and where it fits into a good relationship. But as I interviewed people, they simply said, "Well, yes, of course, we always expected fidelity." Couples who are able to make marriage fulfilling and satisfying simply do not even entertain the idea of an "open marriage" or multiple partners. Couples who contemplate meaningful relationships and are capable of achieving them seem to begin with this given: monogamy is the only way to go.

Remember to let the winds of heaven dance between you.

RALPH BLUM

Figure 16.4. Couple's Dance

17

MAPPING YOUR JOURNEY
OF CHANGE

*D*ivorce often leaves us feeling powerless, but as we have shown here and in one of my previous books *Choicemaking*, we don't have to be victims. Although our ability may become obscured by emotion at times of crises, we never lose the power to change our lives for the better.

As we renew our efforts to make healthy moves in our own and in our loved ones' interests, we observe that we can make successful decisions again. Anyway, being 100 percent right in life is a capacity of perfection that no one enjoys. Not many of us can even predict how we'll change, much less how our spouses will change. So, full of forgiveness for our own shortcomings and others, we find our new way through a new life, brimming with exciting possibilities.

Following a divorce, we are eager to start planning for the future. Then we realize that along the way, in a marriage with many demands (perhaps including those of our children), we've neglected to stock some of the tools we need for self-sufficiency. Maybe we were borrowing others'. Now, though, we recognize some of the capacities that we need to boost our lives forward. They may include the ability to listen, share thoughts and feelings, decide on some healthy new commitments that make us feel good, and learn when and how to ask questions.

Most important, our recovery months are the time to find out how to trust, rest, reflect, and make changes. They are a period in which we have been challenged to simplify and reach some inner peace. After all this, do we get to lean back and cruise on our life's journey? No way! The biggest changes, possibly the hardest ones, and those with the greatest rewards are yet to come!

During this time of self-supportive care, you have been preparing for the most important phase of recovery: The commitment to keep it going, to make self-care, self-development, and self-discovery a continuing effort in your life. Establishing a set of goals will focus you on that promise to yourself.

What Are Your Pro-Self Rights?

One of your prime goals should be to remember to assert your rights at every opportunity. This may take a great deal of practice, but practice will give you confidence in the necessity of living your own life. Many people think the choices they make are their own until they review a basic list of human rights, such as:

1. You have a right to say no to anything that violates your values.
2. You have a right to say no to requests that conflict with your priorities.
3. You have a right to stand up for yourself.
4. You have a right and an obligation to honestly share your feelings.
5. You have a right to change your mind.
6. You have a right to seek healthy feelings and behaviors from others.
7. You have a right to make mistakes.
8. You have a right to your own program of recovery and healing.

Growing Healthy Through Change

For someone who has been watching and waiting for the approval of others, weighing alternatives without acting, stalling in fear, or being paralyzed with concern over making mistakes, choicemaking is a difficult task. As we enter divorce recovery we often expect too

Divorce recovery is possible for those who can make changes.

much of ourselves too soon. Growing healthy means taking more and more responsibility for every area of life, but this good feeling won't come overnight. We will make some mistakes, execute some false starts, have some hesitation, and fall back to gain strength. Push yourself, but don't push yourself down. To learn to swim you first have to learn to float. But in order to learn to float, you have to let go of that familiar bottom of the pool and lean into the water. We have to give ourselves up to something that, at first, feels as if it won't support our weight. But life is supportive; that's its job!

SURRENDER

As we move forward on our path, we will find ourselves repeatedly in situations that require learning and relearning the value of acceptance and surrender. The dictionary defines surrender as the "giving up of one's position." Here's my definition, a little bit more elaborate, of what I've found surrender to be:

1. Surrender means not being protective of other people, but to let those you love face their own reality.
2. Surrender means to stop controlling others and to start using your energy to become what you dream yourself to be.
3. Surrender is to accept and not regret the past, which is done and over with. It is to grow, plan, and live.
4. Surrender is to stop playing games with oneself, to stop denying, and to start seeing things as they are.
5. Surrender means to stop being in the middle of a raging and controlling event. It is to let go.
6. Surrender is to celebrate victory!

The victory of recovery does not come easily. It is preceded by many losses, good-byes, times of loneliness, and sometimes fear. There are many things to think about and, often, too little time. We have new thoughts and new questions. Yet you know you're on the right path because of the moments of inner peace and inner comfort that are beginning to occur more frequently.

Becoming a choicemaker and freeing yourself from emotional bondage allows you to start your passage away from anxiety. When we look back at our marriages from this vantage point, we may see that for some time it was a stagnant pond, familiar yet not too healthy. If you dam up a river, it will die. Life must move on. What is most natural for people, too, is to live and to grow and not to cling to the status quo.

Recovery Pitfalls

The good feelings and growth you will begin to experience in recovery will be necessary to sustain you as you reenter and renegotiate new situations. In this process you will encounter some pitfalls that are important to skip across so your recovery doesn't stall. Here are the most important recovery pitfalls:

1. *Clinging to resentment.* Resentment will bring us back to negativity. Forgiveness and understanding is a part of healing.
2. *Secret recovery.* Downplaying the joy of recovery dilutes it. It's important to share your excitement with family and friends.
3. *Recovery guilt.* Not embracing the fullness of recovery because we feel sorry for those who are still hurting makes us vulnerable to relapse and retreat; this is self-sabotage.
4. *Fear and avoidance.* Knowledge that doesn't lead to action only brings about frustration. We don't need frustration in divorce recovery. To know we need to make a change and

actually changing are two different things. We can't bridge the gap with fear and avoidance. Only action brings about newness in our lives.

RELAPSE SYMPTOMS

If we become mired in any of these pitfalls, we run the risk of prolonged relapse or stagnation in our growth. We need to pay special attention to the following symptoms of possible relapse. Enlist the help of those close to you as lookouts for any of these symptoms. It is much easier to prevent a relapse than to recover from it. Symptoms of possible relapse are:

1. *Fatigue.* This results from allowing yourself to become overly tired or careless about your health. Workaholics, especially, try to do too much too fast in recovery.
2. *Frustration.* Feeling thwarted is only a sign that we're not expressing appropriate anger.
3. *Impatience.* We find ourselves short-tempered when we try to take control again.

12 STEPS BACK TO RECOVERY

If you feel any of these symptoms occurring with regularity, there are some steps you can take to get back into recovery:

1. Make a commitment to seek outside help from a therapist.
2. Ask someone who cares about you for an opinion of how you're doing—and listen to it.
3. Stay with the truth. (No fibbing, understatements, or white lies.)
4. Make obvious decisions.
5. Take responsibility for yourself.
6. Get some exercise and take care of your body.
7. Choose friends carefully. Misery loves company, but it may

not be the best company. Surround yourself with people who have positive attitudes.

8. Accept some down hours and days. Living in sunshine without rain stunts growth.
9. Learn something new. Knowledge is power.
10. Heal family rifts wherever possible. Good family friends are a wonderful support system.
11. Take plenty of time to be quiet and alone. As we continue to know ourselves and spend time with ourselves, we heal.
12. Expect and recognize wonderful surprises. Over time they will become more frequent.

Risk and choicemaking may not be easy, but if you risk nothing, nothing will be gained. The greatest block to recovery is to risk nothing. You may avoid short-term discomfort or suffering, but you will also block learning and feeling, changing and loving, and any kind of a full, exciting life. That is the forfeiture of human feeling.

Only the person who risks is truly free.

DR. LEO BUSCAGLIA

The Rainbow Check-Up

The rainbow has long been a good-luck sign in the life of humankind, representing balance, beauty, and prosperity. Such is the mystical, luminous beauty of rainbows that we have long speculated begin and end in spots very fortunate, containing great wealth or the proverbial pot of gold.

For many years, I was active in a spiritual community called the Cursillo. One of our special symbols of joy and balance was another multicolored entity, the rooster, again signifying the richness of a balanced life.

A way to keep track of how much color and brightness you are bringing to your own life is to chart your self-care monthly with My Rainbow Color Wheel. Purchase a fresh new set of colored markers, and at the end of the month evaluate your wheel. You can make several copies of this page and fill in the different-colored bands to represent responsibility you have taken for yourself. As you accumulate these records, you will gain confidence seeing your life become more colorful and rich.

Figure 17.1. Rainbow Color Wheel

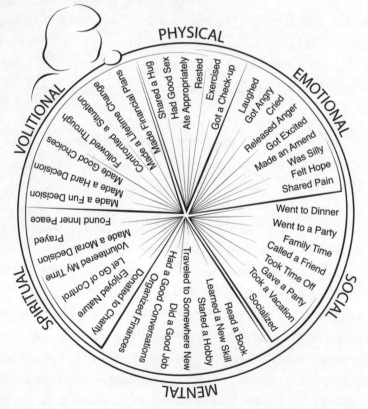

From the Old, the New

What may feel like an end may just be the darkness before the dawn, and that dawn may be a new idea, a new possibility, a new challenge, or a new person. You have within you the power to turn your terminations into transitions, and your transitions into new beginnings.

Sometimes when we think we have to start all over again, we moan, "Oh, my God, I've wasted all of my history, all of my past, and all of my experience." That is a myth stemming from insecurity. Rarely has any of our past been in vain or wasted.

If we can dream it, we can do it. Courage plus commitment plus action result in the confidence it takes to make dreams happen.

Our feelings are our sixth sense. It is this sense that interprets, arranges, directs, and summarizes the other five. Our feelings tell us whether we are experiencing threat, pain, regret, sorrow, joy, or fear. Feelings make us human. Feelings make us all siblings. Because so much of what we know depends on our feelings, not to be able to feel them, identify or talk about them, or to be confused by them is to be overwhelmed by the world. Understanding feelings is the key to mastering ourselves and finding much of our own personal power.

If you allow yourself to experience the natural stages of emotional hurt and do not try to avoid reality, you will be able to resolve your pain and you will heal. Your energy will return and so will your clarity. The practice of facing and solving emotional problems strengthens our ability to achieve real growth and development in life. Otherwise, the unresolved issues of our childhood and of our later crucial experiences will continue to reappear as conflicts in our lives and to shape us in ways we don't want. We can see the purposeful pattern of those who are serious about claiming their share of happiness in life through self-understanding. They move from dependency to independence to mastery to freedom.

If we are closed, we will waste our energy and never attain our potential. If we remain open to new ways of thinking and being, we will grow.

Every ending is a new beginning.

Notes

Chapter 3

1. Gary Small, MD, "Brain Bootcamp," *Psychology Today*, June 19, 2009, http://www.psychologytoday.com/blog/brain-bootcamp/200906/is-technology-fracturing-your-family.

2. Ki Mae Heussner, "Is Technology Taking Its Toll on Our Relationships?" ABC News (blogs), *ABC News*, March 13, 2010, http://abcnews.go.com/blogs/technology/2010/03/is-technology-taking-its-toll-on-our-relationships/.

Chapter 6

1. Pauline H. Tessler and Peggy Thompson, *Collaborative Divorce: The Revolutionary New Way to Restructure Your Family, Resolve Legal Issues, and Move on with Your Life* (New York, NY: HarperCollins, 2006).

Chapter 11

1. *Business Week* (September 30, 1985).

Chapter 13

1. Sharon Wegscheider-Cruse, *Choicemaking: For Spirituality Seekers, Co-Dependents, and Adult Children* (Deerfield Beach, FL: Health Communications, Inc., 1985).

Chapter 14

1. Kathy Ellison, "A Fool and Her Mummy,"
   Miami Herald, April 11, 1993.
2. Kahlil Gibran, *The Prophet* (New York: Alfred A. Knoph, Inc.,
   1923; 1951 by Administrators C.T.A. of Kahlil Gibran Estate
   and Mary G. Gibran).

Chapter 16

1. Sharon Wegscheider-Cruse, *Intimacy and Sexuality*
   (Rapid City: ON-SITE Training and Consulting, Inc., 1991).
2. Sharon Wegscheider-Cruse, *Coupleship: How to Build a
   Relationship* (Deerfield Beach, FL: Health Communications,
   Inc., 1988).

Acknowledgments

$\mathcal{I}$ would like to thank Peter Vegso, Gary Seidler, and Health Communications for originally inviting me to publish this book. To have the opportunity to revise and add to it showed me that Health Communications wants to stay on the forefront of what is happening in our culture, and I am proud to include additional chapters on collaborative divorce, technology, and more. Thank you to Tonya Woodworth for taking this journey with me.

Sharon Wegscheider-Cruse

About the Author

$\mathscr{S}$haron Wegscheider-Cruse is a nationally known consultant, educator, and author of seventeen books, many of which have been translated to French, German, Greek, Japanese, Portuguese, and Spanish. She was the founding chairperson of the National Association for Children of Alcoholics. As a family therapist, she has conducted workshops around the world consulting with the military, school systems, business and industry, treatment centers, and corporations. She is a past winner of the Mary Mann award in recognition for her achievements and contribution to alcoholism communications, and she is the subject of several DVDs used for training purposes. Sharon has appeared on *The Phil Donahue Show*, *The Oprah Winfrey Show*, and *Good Morning America.*. Learn more at www. sharonwcruse.com.